Yes, You!

DELILAH P.I.O.

WESTBOW
PRESS®
A DIVISION OF THOMAS NELSON
& ZONDERVAN

WestBow Press books may be ordered through booksellers or by contacting:

WestBow Press
A Division of Thomas Nelson & Zondervan
1663 Liberty Drive
Bloomington, IN 47403
www.westbowpress.com
844-714-3454

Interior Image Credit: Delilah P.I.O.

Scripture taken from the King James Version of the Bible.

ISBN: 978-1-6642-6073-3 (sc)
ISBN: 978-1-6642-6074-0 (hc)
ISBN: 978-1-6642-6072-6 (e)

Library of Congress Control Number: 2022904791

Print information available on the last page.

WestBow Press rev. date: 06/21/2022

Dedication

Thank you, Lord, for your mercy, providence, and faithfulness in my life and family. I am thankful for your great love, plans, and purpose for my life.

To my two sons, I love you, and I am so grateful to God for giving me you two as my sons. To my son Moses, thank you for having a forgiving, loving, and caring heart. To my son Gershom, thank you for having such a gentle spirit and a kind and giving heart. My sons, you are the most precious gifts in my life, and I am constantly learning from you. God has used you two to teach me how to pray and to not give up on life but to persevere in the faith. Thank you, sons, for putting your faith in God, believing in my words and love, and graciously loving me during all the hardships we had to endure together. I love you both very much!

This book is dedicated to the Lord God the Father, the Son Jesus Christ, and the Holy Spirit.

Contents

Acknowledgments

I start this list of recognition with my grandfather. Thank you, Grandfather Angel, for teaching me the Bible as a child and loving me always. You taught me how to be compassionate by giving me the example of how to live a life committed to God, the family, and others.

I want to thank my parents, Manuel (Don Pachuco) and Asension (Doña Chonita), for giving me the best of you. You have been a great example of how to love unconditionally and how to be a hard worker and brave. Thank you, dear parents, for always teaching me to put other people above the material things in life. Thank you for being an example to follow on how to live with a humble heart.

Thank you to all my brothers and sisters, their spouses, and their children. Thank you for all your support and love, and for always being available for my family and me. I thank God for each one of you and the way you are, how each one has contributed to our family by bringing that sparkle of love, craziness, hard work, happiness, and much more. I cherish the great memories I have of us growing up in our large family. Thanks to the rest of my family. I love you all, and God bless you!

To my husband, my love, thank you very much for supporting me in this job as a writer and for having the patience to give me the time I needed to learn how to become one. The Lord had his plans before we had ours, and I thank him for allowing you to come into my life and for allowing us to fall in love and marry. You are such a blessing! I love you very much!

Thank you to each of my children's fathers for your love and support for our sons. Thank you to the other two children that I helped raise, I love you both very much, and I thank God for your lives. God bless you all!

My Gratitude To

Thank you, Eileen, for being obedient to the Holy Spirit by helping me with my book and making sure you respected my writing style. Also thank you to those who helped me with this book: my nephew Japhet; my niece Jenny, Letishia, Rebecca; and my sister-in-law Leonor.

A special thanks to all my friends in the United States for opening your homes to me and my sons. Thank you, Lisa and family; Drucilla and her son; Maricela and family; Leida and family; Rose; and Lisa and family. God bless you all!

Thanks to each one of you who have been a part of my life. You have left a piece of you in my heart and memories. I start with the Pastors: Cano, Marcos, Daniel, Daniel & Guille, Cipriano, Marcos R., Angel & Chary, Felipe & Jenny, Joel & Kelly, Mike & Hannah, and Abel. The families: Lozano, Alvarado, Zubieta, Ayuso, Zoila, Rosita, Mother Sarah, Dunia & Kevin, Linda & Iran, Ernesto, Claudia, Sergio, Mara, Angelica, Anel, Luz, Lucero, Eunice, Josephine, Marilisa, Lisa, Drucila, Leida, Letishia, Charlotte, Mary, Maricela, Susana, Vanessa, Vicky, Audra & Ron, Dawn & Robert, Tery & Paul, Maura, Lisa, Janet, Denise, Lisa, Rosalind, Isabel & Sergio, Erika, Vincent, James, Emily, Nashielli, Rose, Lisa & Evan, Grace, Oddie, Deborah, Gena, Aida, Nicole, Essy, Hailey. The congregation where my brother Pastor Angel Perez pastored for 18 years, the Nazarene Church Communion in Tijuana, Mexico. You all have been that fresh mist of God over my life when I needed it most, either to be with me in difficult times or to celebrate with me the joyful moments in my life. I love you very much. Thank you all for being in my life, for praying and helping me. God bless you and your families. Proverbs 17:17 reads, "A friend loveth at all times, and a (sister) brother is born for adversity."

My life is a tribute to God for his love and faithfulness, a tribute to my family and their love, a tribute to my friends and their goodness, and a tribute to the church for bringing Christ into my life and their intercessory prayers. God bless you all!

Prologue

I Need to Be Loved!

I was becoming more and more in love with God every day, but at the same time, I was very lonely and hurt because I was going through my second divorce. I had been writing in a journal for barely two months, and this was something new to me. One day when I finished writing, I wrote these words: "No man can satisfy me until I am satisfied with My Great I AM—Jesus! If God has a missionary husband for me, He will provide it, and if not, I accept my singleness."

Despite being in the process of divorce, I still believed in love and longed to be loved by a man and remarry. I really did not think this would happen to me soon, but it did. Seven months after my second divorce, I remarried, thus starting my third marriage. I had met my third husband at my Christian church, and we had gone out a few times thinking we could become friends, and without realizing it, we fell in love and started to date. Soon after this, we became engaged, and months later, we married without really knowing each other.

When we dated, we had problems, but after we married, these issues continued and never got resolved. There were many conflicts, and they almost always ended up with my husband running me out of the house, but I never left the house. Instead, he would leave the house, abandon me for a few days, and then return as if nothing had happened. My life became a cycle of arguments, abandonment, and pain, but I endured everything, pretending that everything was fine between us. I slept in another room to avoid having more conflicts when he was home and in a bad mood or after arguments. It was very difficult to accept the fact that I had failed in another marriage, so instead I tried to fix it—but without much success.

We had many great days, and those were the times when both of us would show love for each other. They were other times when we did not normally talk but live as roommates. The only thing we had in common was that we liked to eat and travel, but apart from that, we were opposites in everything. I knew that only God could help and change our marriage for good. Every time we reconciled, I would pray for us or ask my husband to lead us in prayer, but he was not always willing. I thought things would change, but unfortunately, they did not. Instead, they got worse as my husband struggled with me serving God and working on what I wanted, and I did not understand why.

My position and desire were to remain married, but this meant giving up on serving God and my dreams of the type of career I wanted. When I was his girlfriend, I shared with him that I was going to continue my missionary work and that I was going to finish my degree so I could use it to work helping people, and he had no objection. But now that we were married, he was forbidding me from serving God and work on what I wanted. I only had his permission to be a wife and mother and accept the job he thought was best for me. He wanted full control of my life, all because he was jealous of God and every person with whom I interacted. I was living with such a broken spirit, asking God to change my situation even though it did not improve. I seemed to get worse every day until one day I hit rock bottom!

One day I tried to talk to him about the struggles in the marriage, but things ended in an argument. It seemed as he could not handle this marriage, and in reaction to it, he would do what he normally did. He would leave me. So, he left me but returned the following day to pick up his belongings. After he was through collecting his things, we talked. During the conversation, he said words that hurt me very much that led me to despair. I was already very broken and abandoned, and upon hearing his hurtful words, these led me into the abyss.

I asked myself, "For what was I created? I know I am a mother, but how is it possible that no man can love me? This husband tells me the same things as my previous husband. Why?"

This caused so much devastation in me that I wanted to flee. I thought of bad things, like hurting my own body so I could disappear from this world. I wanted to keep living for my children, but I was in so much pain, and I did not want to hear another man telling me that I was not lovable. I could not bear it anymore! Because I was unable to change my husband and make him love and accept me, I got angry and broke a red vase that I had on my table. I could not believe that these words had come out of the mouth of my husband, the man who was supposed to love me. And then I thought, *I was not born to be loved by any man except by my two sons.*

As a young girl, I always thought that no man should love me, because of everything I lived in my childhood. In this third marriage, I felt that this came true again, but I did not want to accept it until my husband expressed it in his own words on this day, even though his deeds had already proven it. I was already very depressed because of my husband opposing my calling and work, and this put me in a deeper depression. My spirit felt broken. I was in a spiritual drought, which is a dangerous thing.

I thought, *What good is my life? How is all this happening to me? How can this be possible for a person like me, who loves God? I think I am a good mother and wife, so why am I treated this way?*

Thank God that He knows all my thoughts and interceded on this day by allowing my husband and me to calm down and talk. I expressed to my husband that it was wrong for him to speak to me with such cruelty and that I was incredibly sad and hurt. At the end of our talk, he left, as planned. I could tell that my husband felt bad about the incident but had no idea how hurt and depressed he left me.

He returned home on Saturday, and on Sunday we went to church as usual. That day I cried, imploring God to fix my marriage. I told Him that I did not like living like this and that I knew that He didn't like us, his children, living in constant fights. I said this prayer while standing next to my husband at our Christian church during the time of praise and worship. I felt hopeless and without purpose! I did not understand how we could be together in the church, but once the service was over, we could not carry on and live with love. My prayer was a plea to God because I could not keep living in another marital failure. I did not have the strength to fight for one more marriage. I did not understand what was happening to me and us. Where was all the love we said we had when we were dating? I was taking care of myself, my husband, and my children, and the home was well-kept. What else could I do to make him happy? I thought I was like any human being who sometimes had some bad days but not enough for my husband to mistreat me and abandon me. I did not understand.

I burst into tears and asked, "Lord, why am I living? I am lost! I have no purpose. Look at the life I live with my husband. It is one more failure, for the third time!"

At the end of the service, we went home and argued. My husband abandoned me again. For the first time, I was able to tell him before he left, "If you leave, don't come back!"

He left three more times until I finally could say, "No more!" I finally understood that I couldn't change him and that I didn't want to continue living life with a controlling man who had an anger problem. At the beginning of our courtship, I noticed this, but I did not want to acknowledge it. I thought that he would change, but he did not, and I could no longer live like this, like a prisoner. I could no longer live in a place where there was no peace with a husband who refused to change. We could not continue living with such bitterness and unhappiness. So, I would rather be alone with my children and be able to work on what God called me to do in life than to live with my husband fighting every week. I loved my husband and desired to be married, but I did not want to live this way.

After a few days of being alone, I realized the reality of my life and started to cry. I had failed again as a woman, and now I had another marriage failure. I could not accept this again, that I was being abandoned, that I was not wanted and not loved. In my desperation, I went and looked for a friend to comfort me, but I did not find anyone. I went to my church and sought to speak with the marriage pastor, but he was not available. So, I returned home. When I got home, I stopped crying, as I did not want my son to notice. I served him his dinner and spent time with him.

Once he went to bed and fell asleep, I started to cry again. This time I was inconsolable. Then suddenly I heard the voice of God say, "Delilah, stop crying!"

I said, "But, God, my husband keeps leaving me."

God instructed again, "Delilah, stop crying!"

I answered Him, "But, Lord, my husband keeps abandoning me."

God said, "Delilah, stop your crying and fast for seven days because these demons only leave with fasting and prayer! Fast for seven days!"

I then answered God, "Yes, Lord, I will do it!"

I thought, *Of course I will fast! I have been wanting to fast and pray before but did not have the willpower to do it, but no more!*

Get comfortable and join me on this fasting journey and see what the outcome was for my life.

Chapter 1

YES, YOU!

PART ONE
WHO DO YOU CHOOSE?

Remember now thy Creator in the days of thy youth,
while the evil days come not, nor the years draw nigh,
when thou shalt say, I have no pleasure in them.
—Ecclesiastes 12:1

California, February 2, 2017

Day 1 out of 7. Is Thursday, and I begin my first day of fasting and prayer. God leads me to read all these Bible verses:

> For God so loved the world, that He gave his only begotten Son, that whosoever believeth in Him should not perish, but have everlasting life (John 3:16).

> Before I formed thee in the belly I knew thee; and before thou camest forth out of the womb I sanctified thee, and I ordained thee a prophet unto the nations (Jeremiah 1:5).

> For whosoever shall call upon the name of the Lord shall be saved" (Romans 10:13).

God makes me see that despite accepting Him as my Lord and Savior at the age of twelve, my life is not what it used to be at that young age. Today, I am in my early forties, and I see that my life reflects more what the Bible says in Ecclesiastes 12:1, "Remember now thy Creator in the days of thy youth, while the evil days come not, nor the years draw nigh, when thou shalt say, I have no pleasure in them."

This is the Bible verse I had used as the theme verse for my fifteenth birthday celebration, which is known as a quinceañera in the Mexican culture. At this religious ceremony, my pastor prayed for me, and at the end of the ceremony, I was introduced to my church and society as a young lady, according to Mexican tradition.

I can recall being young and not wanting to be in the state that Ecclesiastes 12:1 talks about, nevertheless, today I am in that state, I find no pleasure with my life. When I was a preteen and a teenager, I was full of life and happy, but now in my forties, I am neither happy nor satisfied with my life due to all my marriage failures, including this last one. I am fully satisfied and happy as a mother, but as a woman and wife, I am very unhappy and with much brokenness, all because of my failed relationships with men. I know I had walked away from God when I was nineteen years old, but I returned to him a few years later, and I have been serving Him since. I did not understand. How could I be having another marriage failure?

So, after meditating on all these, I pray, and God answers me right away. He makes me see that He has always loved me, but how I decided to walk away from Him when I was at that young age. That's when I decided who to fall in love with, to do things my way instead of waiting on Him. Also, He makes me see that I am currently disobeying Him.

I ask myself, "Disobeying in what? But if I pray and I seek you. If I am married and I am not just living together with my husband. How is this possible?"

Then I answer myself, "Oh, I know it's because I got married instead of being a writer, and that is my disobedience to God."

I realize what God was talking about. I have been writing down everything He revealed to me, but I never shared them or believed that I should publish them. I know I have failed to do what God instructed me to do.

Since I think I have the answer for God in what I had disobeyed, I pray, "Lord, I disobeyed you. I didn't believe that you called me to be a writer, and instead of doing that, I got married. But now look at me. I am without a husband, and I never obeyed you on publishing what you have given me to write."

Then God replies, "Yes! You disobeyed me. You got married, and you focused only on that! Delilah, the problem is not your marriage! Delilah, the problem is you and your disobedience to me! For when I tell you to do something for me, you do not do it! You got married, and that is not the problem! The problem is that you put aside all I gave you to write. You didn't believe me then, and you still don't believe me now! Delilah, single or married, you have to obey me! Your marriage did not prevent you from obeying me, but You are the one who stopped yourself from obeying me! So now I say Hebrews 12:5 to you. 'My daughter (Delilah), despise not thou the chastening of the Lord, nor faint when thou art rebuked of Him.' I know how hurt and lonely you are because of the failures of your marriages. Your husband is not a mistake. I know how much you need for your husband to love and appreciate you. But first you need to accept my love. Accept me as your husband and be obedient to me."

Then the Lord leads me to read 1 Peter 4:12–19.

Beloved, think it not strange concerning the fiery trial which is to try you, as though some strange thing happened unto you: But rejoice, inasmuch as ye are partakers of Christ's sufferings; that, when his glory shall be revealed, ye may be glad also with exceeding joy. If ye be reproached for the name of Christ, happy are ye; for the spirit of glory and of God resteth upon you: on their part He is evil spoken of, but on your part He is glorified. But let none of you suffer as a murderer, or as a thief, or as an evildoer, or as a busybody in other men's matters. Yet if any man suffer as a Christian, let him not be ashamed; but let him glorify God on this behalf. For the time is come that judgment must begin at the house of God: and if it first begin at us, what shall the end be of them that obey not the gospel of God? And if the righteous scarcely be saved, where shall the ungodly and the sinner appear? Wherefore let them that suffer according to the will of God commit the keeping of their souls to him in well doing, as unto a faithful Creator.

Now I can understand what God was referring to and how my priorities have been wrong. I always wrote everything that God gave me to write, but I kept it to myself and my journal. I could not believe that God would want me to write my life story into a book and publish it. In my mind, I would think, *Who would want to read about the life of a person like me, a person who has failed so much?*

I had more excuses of why I couldn't do what He was asking me to do. I changed my way of thinking, for now God has confronted, and I can admit that I have been disobeying and that's why I have experienced his discipline. Also, I realize that I had hurt my husband.

Why do I say this? Well, I realize now what I did wrong in my marriage. We were just newlyweds when we had our first argument, and after that, I thought that our marriage was a mistake and blamed him for asking me out. On that day, both of us expressed feeling the same way. So, every time we would argue, we would say those same words until our marriage started to fall apart. Clearly, I can see now how I sinned against

God, how I have acted wrong toward my husband, and why this marriage has been so difficult.

God shows me how as a woman I can fall into sin and not realize it until is too late, and he shows it to me with Genesis 3:5–13.

> For God doth know that in the day ye eat thereof, then your eyes shall be opened, and ye shall be as gods, knowing good and evil. And when the woman saw that the tree was good for food, and that it was pleasant to the eyes, and a tree to be desired to make one wise, she took of the fruit thereof, and did eat, and gave also unto her husband with her; and he did eat. And the eyes of them both were opened, and they knew that they were naked; and they sewed fig leaves together, and made themselves aprons. And they heard the voice of the Lord God walking in the garden in the cool of the day: and Adam and his wife hid themselves from the presence of the Lord God amongst the trees of the garden. And the Lord God called unto Adam, and said unto him, Where art thou? And he said, I heard thy voice in the garden, and I was afraid, because I was naked; and I hid myself. And he said, Who told thee that thou wast naked? Hast thou eaten of the tree, whereof I commanded thee that thou shouldest not eat? And the man said, The woman whom thou gavest to be with me, she gave me of the tree, and I did eat. And the Lord God said unto the woman, What is this that thou hast done? And the woman said, The serpent beguiled me, and I did eat.

Who Do You Choose?

> For the flesh lusteth against the Spirit, and the Spirit against the flesh: and these are contrary the one to the other: so that ye cannot do the things that ye would.

—Galatians 5:17

I could see that just as Eve fell, I fell, and I continued to fall when tempted. For when I was at the age to date and fall in love, I was amazed more by man than by God. This leads me to examine my life and see which decisions I have taken. I needed to ask myself, "What have I sought in a man, the spiritual side or the carnal side?" To find out the answer, I had to do the following list.

Graphic 1: Carnal versus Spiritual

Carnal		Spiritual	
Proud	Greedy	Humble	Meek
Rebellious	Evil	Faithful	Joyful
Angry	Unstable	Generous	Loving
Selfish	Fearful	Available	Responsible
Hater	Irresponsible	Self-control	Honest
Insecure	Out of Control	Sincere	With Faith
Liar	Lazy	Has Initiative	Creative
Doubtful	Without Discernment	With Discernment	Discreet
Gossiper	Fickle	Decisive	Alert
Sleeper	Wicked	Compassionate	Wise
Fool	Deceiver	Firm	Attentive
Dishonor	Without Virtue	Obedient	With Honor
Unfair	Dissatisfied	Just	Determined
Unforgiving	Spiteful	Tolerant	Satisfied
Insensitive	Messy	Forgiving	Dependable
Drunken	Rude	Cautious	Keeps his Word
Capricious	Lacks Diligence	Diligent	Friendly
Idolater	Fornicator	Patient	Hospitable
Impatient	Ungrateful	Grateful	Enthusiast
Lustful	Double-minded	Gentleman	Punctual
Unfaithful	Impulsive	Works	Protector
Addict	Jealous	Endures	Virtues
Corruptible	Pervert	Self-confident	Stable
Adulterer	Disrespectful	Giving	Respectful

Delilah P.I.O.

This list made me see some of the struggles of the flesh of some of the men I had dated and how each one of them had contributed to my hurt, so it is their fault that today I find myself suffering. When I was about to finish the list, I realized that I too have struggled with that carnality and not just them. This mind change allowed me to make a list of a spiritual man and see that not every man was bad, but some were spiritual. And those who were spiritual had to struggle with the flesh, just like me.

This made me accept responsibility because I was the one who chose to accept them into my life. Recognizing my carnality and accepting my responsibility led me to see that I had based all my love relationships on my childhood traumas and its consequences. I had never seen this before until now, and this allows me to understand why it did not matter how much I desired to be happily married if I am so broken on the inside. I carry these traumas, which affect me in my relationship with my husband, and these memories of pain and shame did not ever go away. To relive all those moments of my past makes me very anxious, but I know I need to face my past so I can be done with it! I have kept it a secret, and it has kept me living in shame and fear most of my life. But now I must face it so I can experience healing in my life.

I grew up with outdoor toilets only, and this was always a traumatic experience. I was always scared of falling inside. Around the age of five, I was walking in our backyard and did not notice that the septic tank was open. This was where all the dirty water was stored. I was walking and did not notice that the metal sheet was not covering the hole completely, and without noticing it, I fell in the water. I started to scream for help, and an older brother came to my rescue and got me out. Our backyard was very big, and in our large family, everyone was always busy doing something, but thank God my brother heard my cry. I was so filthy when he pulled me out from the sewage. My long hair, dress, and face were soaked with filthy water, and I was so stinky. I was so scared and thought I was going to die. This near-death experience caused me to be afraid of being underwater.

Another time I burned my bare foot with hot charcoal at my mom's outdoor kitchen, and another time I cut my right eyebrow while running around a tractor. I still have the scar to remember it. My mother got so scared that she almost passed out. My sisters and my aunt had to take care of my bleeding eye. Only by talking about those experiences is how I can face and talk about what is so traumatizing to me.

I was born into a large family. We were thirteen in total, including my parents, and I was the second youngest and the youngest girl. I was an outdoor child and a busybody, so when I was not at school, I could be found playing with my siblings, cousins, or kids from the neighborhood. When I was about five years old, a man tried to sexually molest me while I was playing with his daughter. He could not do anything because I managed to sneak out and escape.

At that age, I did not know it was a sexual thing, but I knew that what he was forcing me to do was not normal, so I ran away. But unfortunately, two major things happened to me around the age of five. I was sexually molested, and I heard a voice telling me to chant words and repeat them. It became a game for me, not knowing that it would lead me to change my behavior and cause me to commit sexual sins and other sins.

I was too young to know that this was sinful, but I did know that it was evil. I could not stop it and battled with this for a year. I felt I could not share with anyone what was happening with me, so I kept it all to myself. Then I started to have bed accidents at night. I would wet the bed or hammock while sleeping. I had this problem until around the age of nine, and on many occasions, my father would severely discipline me after noticing my accidents. As if I hadn't had enough of evil things happening to me, eviler things would happen around the age of nine, I was exposed to pornography. All my innocence was lost!

All the things I went through as a child did not stop me from being a child and living a normal life, or so I thought. At the age of nine, we had moved into my fourth home since the day I was born. In this home, we only had two rooms and an outside bathroom, but it was finally a normal bathroom, which made me so happy. We had a small yard, but we had enough space to play and for my dad to have some plants, trees, and chickens. We had a well in our backyard, which we used for all the water needs at home.

We were poor in the beginning years of living here that they were times that for breakfast we would eat a fresh corn tortilla covered with lard and a pinch of salt. And on days when we had nothing, a neighbor would give my mom some food without my dad knowing since he had told her to not ask anyone for help. We lived in a poor neighborhood, so most of the neighbors were poor like us, except that we were one of the largest families in the neighborhood. In my previous neighborhood and in this one, I was being bullied by other children and some adults because I was learning to speak a second language and did not speak it well.

Soon I started getting in trouble at home and even on one occasion at school. My bad behavior was followed by severe discipline from my dad, which hurt me and would get me truly angry. On many occasions, I would take my anger out on one of my sisters, who is a year older. I would come to resent her because she always behaved so well and treated me as if I was her twin. She was a twin but not with me, since her twin was a boy and we were just a year apart, my mother would dress us alike as if we were twins, which I disliked. My father always had me go to the store with her since she was always scared to go alone, and my dad would say that my job was to protect her. I just did not like being her bodyguard.

Occasionally when we were on our way to the store, I would be mean to her, and in return, she would just be kind to me, which would upset me. I could not understand how she could be nice to me after what I had done to her. All I could see in her was weakness, and I did not want to be that way.

My father's severe discipline toward other siblings and I started negatively affecting me, to the point that I started to resent him, which then escalated to hate. Submitting to my dad's authority was hard for me, and oftentimes I got in trouble for rebelling against his rules and him. I was about ten years old, too young to understand what was happening with me and my life, but all I could see was that I was being severely punished. I felt as if my heart were breaking every time my father disciplined me, and out of resentment one day, I said to myself, "I will not cry in front of him. I will not let him see me cry!"

And on that day, my anger became hatred, and I became a little child with mixed emotions toward her father, the man who is supposed to be her most important male role model. These mixed emotions toward my dad and his discipline caused me to harden my heart. It was so noticeable that my own family nicknamed me "Heart of Stone." I was nicknamed before, and I didn't care what I was called, but I just felt that I wasn't going to let any man discipline me. That was the day I lost respect for men.

I became very defensive and started to behave much like a boy, so much so that I was called a tomboy. I played mostly with boys and tried to be very tough like a boy. I liked playing with marbles and other boys' games and cared much about showing that I could play just like a boy. My identity was in confusion. I was a girl, but I wanted to feel like a boy. I had made up my mind that I would never fall in love so no man could hurt me. I would dress as a girl and know I was a girl, but inside of me, I felt my heart of stone was protecting me. So, I kept living that lie.

When it came to making friends, it was easier for me to become friends with boys than girls. Oftentimes I would make fun of how delicate girls were. My brothers and their friends would call me señorita ("young lady" in Spanish) when I was about eleven years old, and that would make me upset. My family used to tease me about boys and would tell me that once I start liking boys, I would care about my looks, but their comments would just make me angry.

Once I reached the age of twelve, I stopped playing much with boys and became more interested in being a girl. At this age, I had already developed physically more than other girls my age, and the boys at school noticed that. Most of the time, I felt treated like an older girl, and older boys and even adult men would try to flirt with me. Due to my body development, I was bullied a lot and called by the name of a burlesque dancer. Occasionally I would arrive home and cry, begging my parents to do surgery on me so I could be normal like the other girls my age. I was so traumatized that I would try to hide that part of my body by wearing three blouses.

Since I noticed that I could not change my body and because of my poverty and the attention I was receiving from men, I then decided I would become a burlesque dancer once I became eighteen years old. So, I thought, because I loved music and dance, I would use my body to make money and be like the burlesque dancers of Mexico that I watched on television. I said to myself, "They use their body to make money. Well, I can do the same." In my mind, I was thinking that this would be the best way to take vengeance on men. Of course, no one in my family or the world knew what I was planning for my future and why, so I thought, but God knew it all.

I knew God existed, but I really didn't understand much about him. As a child, I had been exposed to the Word of God by my grandfather who would read and teach us the Bible. Also, around the age of five or six, a Christian church was started next to my home, and one of my teenage brothers became a Christian. I would go to church with him but never accepted Christ, and I had no idea what it meant to do so. When I went to church, I just liked it because I could play. I stopped going to this church because we moved when I was like seven years old. I did not return to one until I was ten when my Christian brother took me for a few visits. But at the age of twelve, I began to attend a Christian church in our neighborhood, which is when I experienced accepting Jesus Christ in my heart.

This caused a drastic change in my life. I was able to forgive my father completely and just love him. I had to see that for being an orphan at a young age from both parents, he was trying to parent us the best he could. I forgave him for his mistakes that he had made during my younger age. I saw how committed he was to our large family and how he never abandoned us but wanted the best for all his children. This change of heart toward my father allowed me to enjoy a great relationship with him. My heart changed toward my twin sister too, and I forgave her. We got to be closer and then attended the same church and became believers.

Another change that took place at this point in my life was that I learned how to behave like a young lady and not a tomboy, like they used to call me. I accepted that I was created a woman and embraced being feminine all the way! I was still competitive, a talker and energetic, but was changing as God was working on my character, thoughts, and whole being. I no longer had the idea of becoming a burlesque dancer since God had shown me that this was sinful. Now I was serving God in the church choir. I got baptized at the age of fourteen when I really understood what it was to give my life to Christ.

The years went by, and I continued to be involved at church and school. I was popular at both places. But I was still carrying much insecurity inside of me and did not feel worthy as a woman because of what I experienced in my childhood. Inside my mind, I always thought that I did not deserve a godly husband if I were to marry one day. I always wanted to talk to someone about what had happened to me as a child, but I had too much shame and fear. This topic was not discussed in the church or at home growing up, so I could never be helped.

I couldn't avoid it, but I started to have some admirers. I was now fourteen years old. I left my neighborhood Baptist church to attend a Nazarene church with one of my brothers. I changed because my local church was too small and did not have many activities and because I was liking a teenage guy from my brother's church. We became friends, and I got close to him for a short time, but it was a very innocent love, liking and friendship, you could say. We never had any dates or became anything more. It was a short time of just liking a boy for the first time. I attended church camps and was popular. I had the opportunity to meet many good friends and bond with a few.

Almost a year later, I had another admirer and allowed him to start courting me. We lived in different cities and just saw each other at church events. I broke the relationship a week after my fifteenth birthday, and I can recall having his parents ask me if their son had done anything disrespectful for this to happen. I gave them the same answer as I gave their son, that I felt too young to be dating and that I wanted to keep my focus only on school. The short dating period lasting just a few months was very innocent and respectful.

I liked him as a brother more than having him as a boyfriend, and I started to get very worried and scared when I realized that he was falling in love with me. I was too young to know what love was, and since he was a few years older than I was, he was ready for love, and I wasn't. I didn't feel worthy of dating him but was so attracted to his godliness, the music ministry he had, and the missionary family he came from. I had a past that I was so ashamed of that I could not bear the idea of dating him and being married to him one day. I felt he deserved better.

At this same age, I was proposed twice, and I felt really threatened to have older men approach me and pop the marriage question. I was afraid, and just thinking about marriage scared me. How would a man react if he knew my past? Would he reject and mock me? I thought of what would happen if people were to find out. Would they mock and reject me too?

After finishing secondary school, I moved to Cancun, Mexico, to live with one of my siblings. My brother was kind to me, and he provided for all my needs and took me out on tours when he could. I would get to spend time with my other brothers who lived there too. I attended one semester of high school and then was forced to move back to Campeche, Mexico, and continue my education there. I had to go home because in Cancun we had a young neighbor I liked, but he was a bad influence on me. My brother stopped me from going out with him and sent me back home as soon as my semester was over. I was first upset but then rather embarrassed with my parents and siblings because I had to be back home. I let myself be carried away by my attraction to this young man and never considered his bad lifestyle.

I settled back home and continued my education as planned, but I was no longer living with my parents, but with my brother who I attended church with and was married now. Living with my brother was a financial help for my parents and me. It allowed me to continue with my schooling. I helped at home wherever I was needed and focused on school, and then later I was able to get my first job as a secretary.

My sister-in-law came from a pastoral family. She and my brother had a missionary and servant heart with the hospitality. They always welcomed her parents, the pastors, and other missionaries visiting the Nazarene church. I was always eager to hear the testimonies that some of them would share. I felt joy and much peace at their home, and I liked that I did not have to share any food with other siblings. I would eat pancakes and cereal at their home for the first time, along with many other foods.

On the weekends, I visited home sometimes but always returned to my brother's, except for some holidays. By now, I only had few siblings left at home, and my parents were not home as much because they would spend a few months visiting the older siblings in Cancun. I spent over two years living at my brother's, and they became my second parents and spiritual parents. Besides attending church with them, I was involved in serving and attending church events, including mission trips. While living in their home, God would bring so many spiritual blessings to me, and one was my calling.

I held various jobs in Campeche, from my first at the age of nine as a part-time nanny and housekeeper to then working as a shoe store attendant. I then worked for a few years at a pharmacy, and my lost job was as a secretary at a supermarket. My father worked various jobs and never had any benefits since he worked as self-employed. My mother was a stay-at-home mom, and all children had to get a job to contribute to the household expenses. All the money earned was given to my father so he could manage it and provide for us.

Once my siblings got older, they all left home but still contributed financially to help my parents. This is how we helped my parents, and this was what meant to be part of our family. I did not get to keep most of my salary until I was around seventeen years old. My salary was only enough to pay some of my bus fares for school, church, and work and contribute to living expenses at home. Once a day, I had to walk to work and school and on few occasions to church, and all this was done in an extremely hot and humid climate, but it was my only choice.

I made so little money that for my first Christmas as a young eighteen-year-old lady, I had to save money for a whole year to buy myself a new dress. Oh, this dress was not from a boutique, but it was a dress I purchased at the market because that was all I could afford. This was the first time in my life that I had purchased something big, expensive, and just for me. When it came to accessories, my youngest sibling would spend the little money he would make and buy earrings for my "twin" sister and me.

For New Year's, I could not afford to buy anything so my brother, the one I lived with, gave me a present, a piece of fabric. With this piece of fabric, I hand-made a dress and purchased more material, and I made my jacket to go with it. I used it for my last New Year's in Campeche. At this dinner was where I said goodbye to my church youth group since I had made plans to move to Tijuana, Mexico. If I hadn't known how to make my dress, I would have had to use my usual clothes for this special day, and my clothes were pretty worn out since I shared them with my sister, the twin.

With my parents' permission, at the age of eighteen, I moved from Campeche to live in Tijuana with my older sister. I was not raised with television, and my family did not get one until I was around fourteen years old. We did not have many books and were not a reading family, except for one of my brothers, who was a teacher. So reading was not a habit, and the only books we had at home were textbooks, comics, or some magazines. Around the age of ten, my brother, the teacher, purchased a set of encyclopedias, and with it came a book that had pictures of movie actors and actresses from America and Europe. I was dazzled when looking at all the photos of famous people, and on this day, I decided to dream of one day traveling and seeing the United States and the rest of the world.

So, I moved to Tijuana to help my older sister with the care of her two little girls, as one of them was born with a disability and needed more care than the other one. Also, I moved to fulfill my desire for better employment and life, to fulfill my dream of traveling and seeing the world.

The change was not easy. I had to get used to living in a different climate and living without an income. I had committed to helping my sister full time for a whole year. In return, she provided me with a place to sleep and food and gave me a ride to church or money for my bus whenever she could afford it. She lived with her two daughters and their father, all on a one-family income. As soon as the year passed by and I was no longer needed, I got a job. This brought me an income and independence. Then I got a better job and was able to get my U.S. visa and fulfill my dream of traveling. I visited California every time I could since Tijuana borders with California.

I then had my first boyfriend around the age of twenty, but this relationship led me to fornication and to struggle with my walk with God and church attendance. I ended that relationship and would feel bad about my sin, but my guilt would not allow me to be consistent in going to church. Therefore, I would not attend church so often, and I would just feel condemnation because of my guilt. I never felt connected with most of the congregation, so leaving the church was not hard for me. Before I moved to Tijuana, I was well-known at my church back home where I was continually active, but at this new church, no one knew me. I felt so out of place. So, I thought that it was best to just walk away from the church, even though they always welcomed me.

And it was not just at the church that I felt that way, but it was about my life in the city that I was having problems too. I never felt at home in this city but felt so alone and constantly missed my family, friends, home, and way of living. But despite all the discomfort and disconnection, I decided to remain in Tijuana and not give up on my dreams.

My sister moved to another city, but I stayed in Tijuana to keep working. I started suffering from anxiety and tried to calm my nerves. I consumed a lot of sweet food. This anxiety was something new to me, and I did not know how to cope with it. Although the sweet food did not help me, at least I felt that I blew off steam this way. I was a young lady and an easy target for sexual harassment, and one of the places that it happened was at work. My friendly, talkative personality oftentimes gave the wrong perception to men who were after something else.

This incident at work overwhelmed me and filled me with much anxiety that it sent me to the hospital where I was diagnosed with a severe colitis attack. What led me to be so sick was that I indulged in so much sweetbread and cookies to try to calm my anxiety. I did not lose my job but was transferred to a different department after I spoke with the manager about the harassment. I needed my job, and there was nothing else I could do. The law could not protect me, so I had to just move on and pretend that it never happened.

From this day on, this type of food became my addiction and escape to try to calm my nerves and anxiety. And although the excess of sugar never affected my weight, it did impact my health, bringing me more anxiousness, constantly battling with colitis attacks, but I could not stop eating like this.

When it came to love, I was heartbroken. I so much wanted to be loved by a man and have a family, but this wasn't happening at all. So, at the age of twenty-one and heartbroken, I made up my mind that if I did not get married at the age of twenty-five, I would be single. My idea was that if I was not married at the age of twenty-five, I would adopt a child so I would not be alone. I also felt I would not need any man to help me raise the baby. I continued to work full time, but at the age of twenty-four, I started a new relationship and moved in to live with him. I stopped working and focused only on our relationship since we were planning our wedding. This was the first time in my life that I fell in love and got engaged. I was looking forward to being married and having a family. Sometime after, we were living together, and we were faced with the fact that we could no longer afford our apartment rent, so we had to move into a motel.

Two weeks after living in this motel, I had to make plans to sleep on the streets. I decided that I would move to my old neighborhood where I lived before my engagement, although I was afraid because I didn't feel it was safe to do so in a big city like Tijuana. After I paid my bill and checked out from the motel room, the receptionist asked me if everything were okay with me. He told me that he had noticed that I was always alone. I would go out every day on foot to buy food at the store, and that is how he had noticed that I was alone. I could not hold back anymore and started to cry. I shared that I was no longer engaged and without a place to live and any money.

I told him I was going to get a job right away, but I needed a place to stay in the meantime, but I did not have the money to pay. Since I had stopped working, I no longer had an income, savings, and family to stay with but would have to face homelessness. To cover the room cost, I had to sell my few valuable things I had and kept the rest of my bags with my personal stuff. I was now alone with no money but a few bags and without a home. I thought about going back home to live at my parents' house, but I felt I could not do it. My pride would not allow me. Failure was not an option for me, along with going back home. That is what it would mean to me, that I was a failure. I was too young to fail, and I could not give up so easy. So, I decided to remain in Tijuana.

The receptionist felt sorry for me and offered to help me the way he could, to stay at the motel. He risked his job and helped me this way. I could stay in a room, but I would have to vacate it as soon as it was needed for the client. I was happy to accept his condition and thanked him for helping me. He kept my belongings in his office while I slept in rooms before they were occupied and after the client left without anyone noticing. This was normally in the middle of the night. I felt safe because I didn't live on the street, and I was at peace knowing that this gentleman felt sorry for me and was helping me have a place to sleep for a few hours. I had never been without a place to live, as I had always worked in an office and earned enough to support myself, but now I was begging for a place to live. This was the lowest I had ever fallen in my life. This housing situation was so unreal for me, and I needed to urgently get out of it!

I looked for work right away and was able to get a job that same day even, though it was only temporary, and I wasn't going to get paid until two weeks later. I still could not afford to rent a place to live. After my second week of work, I got a place to live in a co-worker's house. I lived with her family, who welcomed me as if I were family.

At the end of my temporary work, I looked for another full-time job, and at that job, I met someone who fell in love with me and desired to court me. I knew I was not ready for courtship, as I was so shattered by what had happened in my previous relationship. Even though I saw this as an opportunity to finally have what I so much desired, which was to get married, have a family, and a home. I was honest with him and shared what had happened in my previous relationship, although he did not deem it important. We began dating, and both thought it would work because we were both Christians and desired the same, to have a family. We then moved in together, and months later we got married. Within months of my marriage, my dream came true. I got pregnant with my first child and was going to be a mother for the first time!

During our courtship, I had returned to the Christian church and continued to attend with my husband when we married. Also, we attended his Messianic Synagogue in San Diego and while attending, I felt the need to return to the mission field. With our contribution and the donations of some members from the synagogue, we were able to help a mother and her newborn in Tecate, Mexico. I then visited that family, accompanied by my younger brother, who was studying to be a pastor.

On a second occasion, I visited and dropped off donations for my brother and other students at the Christian seminary. Even though it was just these two trips I did during this marriage, I was truly blessed because I missed doing mission work so much. The last mission trip I had done before was when I was seventeen years old. When I did the mission work as a youth, it did not involve donations, but I was just visiting the small missions and singing in the choir. So, this was the first time I had asked a church to donate for the mission work, and God used the Jewish Messianic Synagogue to help me return to the mission field.

I attended the synagogue, but it was all new to me, and I did not really understand Hebrew. The service was bilingual, Hebrew and English, but I did not comprehend much, so I would just listen and try to follow with my Spanish Bible. I tried to learn Hebrew, but I could not. I was married at this synagogue, and this was my first time attending a church in the United States and being exposed to the Jewish religion, community, and culture.

I started to have marriage problems, and it did not help us that we were always too busy working, which did not give us much time for us. I was a wife and mother of a newborn, and I was working full time in our business and starting college. To make matters worse, the business had us driving a great deal and crossing the border many times. I very often felt that the world was collapsing on me, and it was hard to get used to living in America. Our communication was not good, and we often had culture clashes, as we were from different countries. I experienced much fear and anxiety sometimes. I did not know how to make things change in my marriage, and in my desperation, I felt as I could not handle it anymore!

So, after two years of marriage, we separated and divorced. My decision to divorce not only destroyed my marriage but also left me with no place to live with my son. When I left my husband, I only took my baby and our small personal belongings. I had to start over in California, where life was more expensive, and I had no family support. I could not leave the country since we had a child together. I had no income and was homeless again, and my only option was to live in a shelter with my son until I could get a permanent home for us to live.

About a year later, I moved out with my son from the shelter into a program that provided us with a low-cost apartment. I got a job to pay for my apartment and continued going to college. I was the only one that supported us financially. Everything was going well, but unfortunately, I felt alone again and in need of a man's love. I started a courtship while fighting the custody of my son, and this was not a good idea since my life was so complicated, but at that time, I could not see it. We had a long-distance relationship since he lived in another state. We only saw each other three times, but on our second visit, I got pregnant with my second child. I was so happy to be pregnant with my second son! This relationship did not work but ended during my pregnancy. He wanted to marry me, but he had asked me to give up being a mother, something I could never do, so I ended the relationship. I could not just keep one child and give my other child away; both of my children needed me and had the right to have me as their mother, and I could never live without my children.

I was incredibly pleased with my decision to keep my son and my second child that was on his way as well. I would rather be a mother than a woman! And I've never regretted that decision, and it's one of the best decisions I've ever made in my life! Although it was very difficult, I remained the only person to support my home even after this second pregnancy, and during this time, I started to learn about faithfully giving my tithings to God despite my needs. I saved as much as I could, and during my second month of pregnancy, I moved to live in Cancun. I returned in hopes of living a better life with my children and being close to my family, but my plans did not work!

That is right. My plans did not work, and instead I had to go through a major trial after having my second son. This was due to bad decisions I had made when pregnant with my second child, and it caused me separation from my two children. Losing them was extremely hard for me and an awfully hard pain to cope with. I finally had one of my sons back with me, and I was able to move back to San Diego, but I had to stay in a shelter again. About a month later, two good friends from church opened their home to us. They took turns hosting us until I could get a job and a place to live. It took me a few months, but God provided a full-time job and an apartment to live in, and I immediately brought my second child to live with us. It was exceedingly difficult for me to be a single mother now of two children because we had no family in the United States, but I never gave up. I worked and supported my children as best as I could, working long hours, using public transportation, and on many occasions walking so I could make my money last longer.

I was the sole provider for my home; therefore, I had to stop studying and work full time. Months later and with much sacrifice, I was able to buy a vehicle in payments through bank financing. I had no credit history and no debt, so I thought this was good, but I soon found out that it was bad when it comes to credit history. I was given the highest interest rate, but this was my only way to purchase a car and make life better for us.

When I needed help with my children, two families cared for my children while I rested or went grocery shopping. On many occasions, I simply needed to be in fellowship with a family, and one of the families offered us that by getting together on the weekends to eat. My ex-husband also started helping financially and spending time with both of my children, not just our son. They were times where he would just take our son only, and I would get to spend that weekend with my baby. On the weekends, we attended church, and I felt that we were finally living a stable life. We attended the mid-week service where I helped in the children's ministry.

Sad to say, I still felt very lonely as a woman and desired so much to be loved by a man. I also longed for my children to be loved and have a father at home so we could be a complete family. My baby was like fifteen months old when I felt that I was ready for courtship and to get married.

I felt that my past was over and that I was ready to be happy and make someone happy too.

I soon met someone, and we started to date. Then we moved in together. Months later we married, and so I started my second marriage. I was in my early thirties, and I was happy that I was no longer alone. Now I had a husband, and my children had a stepfather. Now with my husband, we could support and grow our four children since he had two children as well. Now we were a blended family and instantly a family of six with three different cultures. This meant a lot of work and adjustment, but we tried our best to make it work. Oftentimes when we went out shopping or to eat, people would stare at us, and we were asked questions, like if I had a daycare or if the kids were adopted, because they did not believe we were one family. I kept working full time and dedicated myself to my husband and our four little ones. We had a seven-year-old girl, two five-year-old boys, and a two-year-old boy. Despite thinking I was ready for this family, I was not prepared for all the difficulties that it would entail to have and grow a blended family, especially after all I had lived in my life, but I could not see it until I was married and faced with many challenges.

Months after we married, I stopped serving in the children's ministry because it was best for the family. While dating, we agreed on not having any cable services but to rent movies only on some weekends so most of our time would be focused on our kids. Since the beginning of our relationship, we hardly spent any time alone but always included all the kids on our dates. We both worked full time, and our daily routine was to gather at dinnertime to pray, eat, and spend time as a family. Then the kids would do homework, shower, and then say a prayer before bedtime. Then all went to bed, but we did not spend much time alone as a couple.

I loved spending time with the kids, but I so much desired to go on dates with my husband and take a break from motherhood for a few hours and just relax. My husband became a believer while dating me, and so now we all attended my Christian church.

Despite the hard work that we put into our family, we started to have difficulties as a couple. It didn't help us that we had just gone through a major problem as a couple, but I couldn't get over it. This problem affected me greatly and contributed to me being depressed for a few months. At home, I would feel overwhelmed and have much fear and anxiety. And I would have the feeling of being a failure as a wife, mother, and stepmother. I would spend many Saturdays obsessively cleaning and rearranging the furniture at home, feeling that this would help me feel better since indulging in sugar did not satisfy me anymore! I could not understand my depression because I was so happy to be married and have a family, but on the other side, I felt that this new life was just too much for me to handle.

My depression was hard on my husband. The kids didn't really feel it since I took care of them as usual, but only my husband got to see me in this state of mind, and he felt hopeless just like I did. One of the struggles I had as a parent was that I was too disciplinary and did not know how to let go and just extend grace to the kids, my husband, and myself. There were few instances where I felt I was becoming disciplinary just like my father, and I did not like that feeling. Also, during these circumstances my pain and guilt for having lost my children came afloat. I did not even know I was still carrying those feelings until I went through this depression.

I would wake up in the middle of the night crying with much guilt, feeling I was not being a good parent to our kids. To help me, my husband suggested I go visit my younger brother on the weekend since he knew how much I missed my family and Mexico. This brother was now married and pastoring a church in Tijuana.

My husband felt that my visit to Tijuana would be his last resource in trying to help me since he could not. He felt that the visit would stop me from being so negative about everything in my life and stop me from complaining and having self-pity. I did not know how to change my way of thinking and get rid of my nightmares and the oppression I felt. I believed I was going crazy to the point where I felt I was demon-possessed, and my childhood memories were so vivid again. I was struggling with my mind, just like when I was a young child.

So, I called my brother and shared what I was experiencing, and I went to visit him on the weekend. He and another pastor prayed for me and assured me that as a believer we cannot be demon-possessed. That gave me much peace, but I had feared having those thoughts again. The trip also gave me the family connection I was missing. I then returned home relaxed, along with a new perspective and the desire to visit my brother again.

We decided as a couple for me not to continue working full time but part time, and this helped me ease the overwhelming feelings I would have. My thoughts started to change, and I no longer was having evil nightmares or thoughts. I was no longer feeling oppressed in this way. I began to attend women's Bible study because now I had time, and soon I went to my first and only women's conference. At the end of this event, I opened up publicly when it was prayer time and shared that I was struggling with depression. I got prayed for, and two friends reached out to me. This event helped me set aside my pride and connect with ladies from my church. It brought me a sense of community.

I used to think that I did not need to attend Bible study because I did not know the ladies and did not feel culturally connected, but at the event, I realized I was wrong. We are all women, and all go through changes in our bodies and lives, like the speaker who shared how her life changed, and the struggles that come with it. After this event, I went home and prayed, realizing I been a believer for so long and I was not willing to let go of God but would focus on changing my life.

Right away the Lord showed me what was causing my depression, and that night I was completely delivered from depression. One of the things that God showed me was that I needed to start my day with him, doing my prayer and reading the Bible in the morning and not at nighttime. Usually, I would try to pray and read the Bible at nighttime in bed, but since I would be so exhausted, I would normally fall asleep. God showed me that I needed to give him my day before I lived it, which meant in the early morning, not at a later time when I had already made decisions and done things my way.

Also, he showed me that I had my kids with me, so I no longer needed to fear losing them again. I needed to let go of my pain and enjoy them and live my life. He warned me that if I did not let go, this could destroy me. So, I did as the Lord showed me and let go of the pain of losing my children and the fear of thinking that it could happen again.

Another change I experienced was the changes I was making in my parenting style. God slowly started to break down the wall dividing me from having a better relationship with our children. My husband helped me in this area too, as he was so easygoing and more patient than I was. He helped me to start developing a friendly relationship with the kids and be more gracious with them, which helped me to be more relaxed.

This was not easy at all because I was not raised that way. I was raised in the days where you had to keep a distance between parents and any adults and do as you were told to do, obeying without asking questions. As a child, I had struggled with that way of thinking and would express my thoughts about it, which would cause me more discipline from my father. And that was the same way I was trying to raise my kids, but no more! Now I was learning to give the kids a voice and extend grace to them and myself, but with my husband, it was much harder.

After a few visits to Tijuana, I realized how blessed I was and that they were many people who were less fortunate than I was. I wanted to change that. This impression on my heart caused me to share it with my husband. Now my thoughts were new and good. I wanted to see what we could donate to help others in Tijuana, and my husband was happy for me and agree on seeing how we could help. We looked at what we could donate from what we had at home and made the kids part of it. Each one had to find toys to give away, and they had to be in good condition.

I went through our closets collecting good clothes and blankets and purchased food to donate. We gave a small monetary help to my brother. Now I was no longer depressed but ready to see how to support my brother and his community in Tijuana through the mission work. I started the mission trip alone, and then the whole family joined me. The kids loved being in Tijuana, and they always looked forward to eating tacos. Two years after doing all these trips, I started to ask friends, neighbors and business companies for donations. I soon stopped working part time, and I was just dedicated to my family and the mission work. We became a missionary family. My husband would play his trumpet and lead the worship. He would play with the kids while I directed, organized, and supported the whole program alongside my brother.

Our children helped us load and unload the donations, playing at the outreaches with other kids, serving food, cleaning up, and giving donations away. We started doing outreaches only with the local church, but then the mission work increased so we started helping churches, missions, senior homes, an orphanage, and even medical outreaches. Our home became "God's warehouse" a food bank That is what I called it. We had a room set up to store donations and used some space in our garage too. We always parked our cars in the garage, and I had given my word to my husband that

I would not allow this mission work to affect our family settings. Having the extra room allowed me to keep my home as normal as possible without compromising our living spaces and losing our home cleanliness and order. I learned fast on packing, organizing, unloading, and loading donations so they could fit in my space at home and in the vehicles.

While my husband was at work and my children were at school, I would pick up or drop donations so I could care for my family and make them a priority. We used all our resources and money to care for our family and then for the mission work. We were faced with many hardships while doing the mission work, especially me, but I had to keep obeying God. He had called me to do this work and not men, so I was responsible for obeying him. Also, as a family, we were determined to not allow anything to stop us from doing the mission work, trusting that God would provide as he always did. The Lord would not allow my family to carry all the burden of the mission work, so he intervened.

After five years of being a missionary family, I was given the opportunity to share about our mission work at our church. Soon after that, we had people join us in our mission work and were able to help more ministries in Tijuana. People of our church kept getting involved by donating for the mission work, and many joined us on these trips. Oftentimes they had the blessing of giving the donations directly into the hand of those in need and developing a bond with them. We kept using our home, and through our "God's Warehouse," we had the opportunity to help Mexico, but we were also helping families in our community who were in much need here in Oceanside and its surrounding areas.

I continued leading the mission work with the help of my husband, and we were seeing the impact in the mission field and of the mission workers. I joined the workforce again, but it was not stressful because I was working part time and at the school where my kids were attending. I was a high school Spanish teacher at a Christian school. I shared my mission work with students and that church, and soon many joined us in the mission field. My husband had desired to join the military but knew that if we joined, we would have to leave our home and live wherever he would be stationed. I had not agreed with this choice until God made me see that I needed to submit to my husband who was trying to provide for us.

It was difficult for me to leave my home, friends, and community, but the saddest thing was to leave the missionary work in Tijuana, especially because no one took over our mission work. I obeyed God and agreed with my husband to take this new job. He joined the military and was gone for around nine months on his military training, but weeks before his departure, we faced many challenges that put a further distance between us.

To not let it bother me, I held everything back and remained strong so I could care for my family but feared the estranged relationship we were growing to have. My husband knew the separation was going to be hard but did not realize what I truly was feeling and fearing but was focused on his new job responsibilities. I thought that upon his return we would work on our marriage, never knowing that his return would bring great changes and more separation between us.

Once he returned, he gave me the news that we were going to be living in Germany and that he had to depart in two weeks. So, we said goodbye to the church in Tijuana and stopped all the mission work but committed to keep supporting my brother, the pastor, financially.

My stepchildren stayed with me while my husband was in training and then eventually moved to live with their mother. Meanwhile I was at home with my two sons since soon we would be joining my husband overseas. My move to Germany took six months due to unforeseen issues. I had no choice but to wait with our luggage and sleeping bags since all our belongings had left when my husband departed. These sleeping bags were our bed, and we thought it would just be for a week. And every week we would say, "Maybe this week we will fly" and so on until six months passed.

My youngest son would have nightmares and cry, missing my husband. This was very tough, but I kept assuring him that we were not staying behind and that we would soon be together as a family. I had two great friends, our neighbors, who constantly checked on us and provided anything needed during our wait time. They even offered furniture. I had to decline the furniture since I wanted to be ready to go and not feel like I was staying. I had other friends from church who prayed and helped us too during this waiting time, a tough time.

I promised my children that I would make it up to them for these hard times and we would just enjoy our time while we live in Europe, including traveling. Since we were still in California, I got to spend more time with my stepchildren, friends, and neighbors. While waiting for my move, I had asked God to use me in Germany. I felt in my heart the need to help encourage women and their families to overcome things in life, although as a woman I didn't feel like an example and didn't understand why I had prayed that.

I finally left California with my two sons and flew to Germany, and upon our arrival, we were mesmerized by the beauty of the country and the white snow. My husband was no longer waiting for us because he had deployed, but he had the home ready for us. Finally, we could sleep in our beds! We remained in communication whenever it was possible for him, and I shipped him boxes with many treats, souvenirs, and letters from the kids and me. Within a few months of my arrival, I had to face the beginning of the break-up of my marriage, a very difficult time. I tried to keep myself busy, but I could not do missionary work. So, I was home alone for many hours while the kids were at school.

I was so disturbed by what I was going through, and I could not accept it. This was keeping me awake at night, and it was affecting everything else in my life. I was so puzzled. Why would God allow me to move if this were waiting for me? Why? I was away from home and friends and living in a foreign country with my children. Why did this have to happen so far away from home?

On one of the nights that I could not sleep, I heard the voice of the Lord. He spoke to me about the condition of my broken heart and how he was the only one who could heal me.

He said, "Give me your heart, and I will make it solid and complete, a heart that has no footprints of pain although it has been broken! Only give me your heart, and I will comfort you and fill you with joy. No one will ever be able to see the marks of those pains caused by those who hurt you. People will see a whole heart, as if you have never suffered. Man does not have the capacity or power to heal, but I do! I have the power to give you that whole heart, a healthy heart that even if it is offended or humiliated, hurt, and despised, will remain complete! A heart, although unwanted, can feel love, if loved by the only one who loves your soul, Jesus Christ!"

With this revelation, God showed me two hearts: a broken heart and a complete heart. This would be the first time that I would hear God talking to me in my adult life. The first time I heard Him calling me was when He called me to the altar when I received my calling at the age of sixteen. I have heard of God's will and direction through prayers, but this was different. I was hearing the voice of the Lord speaking to me. To hear God's voice again and the words He spoke to me gave me the strength to endure the difficulties I was facing and what was to come.

A short time after this encounter with God, I would hear Him again. This time was about how I had forgotten who I was as a person and my own needs. He made me see that before I took on these roles in life—a missionary, wife, and mother—I was Delilah, a person who had been born with a name and who had needs to be met. He showed me that I used to enjoy doing things and learning like when I signed up as a teenager to learn how to do crochet.

This revelation of the Lord got me to start paying more attention to my human needs and how to go about meeting them. Normally I was particularly good at helping others with their needs, but I was not very good at caring for my own. I was always busy working and did not rest much or spend much time on myself.

Do not get me wrong. I did take care of myself when it comes to getting dressed, looking clean, and wearing makeup when needed, so it was not about this. Regarding the mission work, I was always busy working, but I was spending so little time being in the Word and worshipping God. I had spent more time helping people rather than taking care of myself. It was not bad to help others. The problem was that I hardly left enough time to take care of all my needs, like spending time making friends, so to speak. I did not prioritize my needs, but I was always at the bottom of the priority list. So, I started to make changes and worked on spending more time reading the Word, praying, and being part of the women's Bible study and not just the Sunday service.

As soon as I arrived in Germany, I made new friends, but now I was making time to really be a friend and spend time with them outside of the church or the kids' school. I got involved in my community, but I was now careful on how much time I volunteered, always being aware of not going over the limit because now I had a limit, which I never had before. I knew I had to keep myself accountable to God, so I was being careful with my time and how I spent it.

I had to face the areas where I lacked as a wife and mother, which was extremely hard to accept, but I had to do it. In this process, I had to learn to know how to not just be a giver but to learn to receive too. I have always been a giver and was so used to giving, so it was hard to learn to accept. This wasn't because of my pride; it was because I felt that there was no need to spend money on me when I could use it to care for my family or the mission work. I used to feel guilty about spending money on me or the family when I could use that money to do mission work. I was now seeing how I failed my family because oftentimes I took from our family finances and provision to give to the needy, not realizing that my family needs should have been first.

Having a home and living with the necessary commodities at home made me think that our needs were not as urgent as those of the people in need, I couldn't see that my family should have been first because my first ministry was my home. I was guilty of not being that affectionate with my husband and of oftentimes not accepting his affections. I was holding too many things against him.

One of the things was that I wanted his time and attention. I had a strong desired to connect with him. Since we did not spend much time together, I was resenting him, which caused me to not accept his affection many times and made me struggle on giving grace and affection to him. I worked on changing my relationship with my husband, but it was hard because our communication was limited due to his being out of the country. My only hope was for when he would return.

In the meantime, I worked on changing the things I could about myself. I was starting to spend time and money on my urgent needs. I had to also learn to spend money on my family, and one of the ways I did was by having fun and traveling. The desires of my heart would be fulfilled. I was now in the middle of Europe, so I took advantage of that opportunity and traveled to other countries. I traveled with my two great companions, my sons, and fulfilled my promise made to them in California of traveling. I participated with my sons in many outreaches that the military offered to us, the family dependents, to help cope with the soldier's deployment. My sons participated in sports and various events offered by the school and after-school programs. I attended many of their sports events. We did miss home and friends, but we were focused on making the best while we lived here.

A good friend from my church back home came to visit us with her daughter, and the five of us traveled together. Their visit brought us a piece of home. My husband was gone for almost a year before he returned from his deployment, but by now we had been physically separated for two years. Upon his return, we tried to start working on repairing the marriage, but we lived in separate rooms and had separate lives. His relationship with the kids was the same, but our relationship as a couple had changed. We were no longer a couple. This was too hard for me to accept, and I could not cope with that. I had left everything to be next to him, and now there was no "us."

Seven months after my husband returned, we left Germany and moved back to the United States. We were stationed in a military base in a small town in Missouri. I came with the same attitude and encouraged my children to do the same, to enjoy this place and make the best of it. I kept working on myself and the things that God had showed me while living in Germany. I remained devoted to my children and the family, but our life as a couple was the same, living separate lives because our marriage did not improve. Since this was going on for a few years, it was causing some bitterness and much pain in me because I wanted my marriage to work. I saw the need to keep going to counseling to help me with my marriage brokenness. I had attended counseling with a chaplain in Germany, so I was now doing the same in Missouri when I needed it.

I kept seeking God and asking him to help me forgive, to have acceptance, and to move on with my life, and I did. I volunteered at a few military community events and became a teacher for the first time at a women's Bible study. That helped me put my eyes on God and brought much growth in my spiritual life. I had chosen to teach a class on prayer when I was given the choice of which book to do. Teaching this class taught me how much I did not know about prayer. I attended mostly a local church, a Baptist church. They had great teaching of the Word and fellowship. This church reminded me of my first Baptist church in Campeche where I accepted Christ. Living in Missouri gave me a closer heart for America. It gave me patriotism, something I did not have before since I did not know much of its history and culture until I lived here.

One day the Lord gave me Isaiah 60:1–2, "Arise, shine; for thy light is come, and the glory of the Lord is risen upon thee. For, behold, the darkness shall cover the earth, and gross darkness the people: but the Lord shall arise upon thee, and his glory shall be seen upon thee."

My life was changing. I was experiencing God's peace and joy even though I was living in a broken marriage. One day while I was exercising at home, I had the idea about writing a missionary book. I kept thinking, *If I could just encourage someone, someone who is going through trials like me, it would be great to help them.*

I knew I was blessed when I helped others, and serving saved me from feeling pity for myself, but instead I would put my eyes on Jesus and showing love to people. Soon the Lord brought a person for me to help. She was a military wife, just like me. I spent months teaching her, counseling and helped her overcome and heal many areas of her life, and I was so blessed by it. This made me think, *If only I could write a book of testimonies from all the mission work I had done through the years and use it to encourage others, this would be great!*

I had never written a book, and the only thing I had written in my life were flyers and newsletters for the ministry. Amazing how God works in our lives, he was the one putting the desire in me to become a writer. I just did not know it yet!

In the winter, I brought my mother to visit us. She was a widow by then, and she stayed with us for three months. I shared with her what was happening in my marriage, and she never intruded but respected me as she had always done and just loved on all of us. On this visit, I got to know her like I had never known her before. I was able to spoil her, something I could not afford to do before even though I desired it. We cooked, did crafts, and went out for dinner. We went to the movies, women's Bible studies, and church. We attended community events, and I got to see her dance with one of the soldiers at the Christmas military dinner. She helped me cook for this event too. I was so happy to see my mother enjoying herself, and I was so proud of who she was. My mother had accepted the Lord as her Savior a few years back, so it was nice to fellowship and pray together, enjoying all these new experiences for her and me. I was blessed to be the one doing it with her, her youngest daughter. On this visit, we cooked together family recipes I had wrote down so I could have them and pass them on to my kids.

Since I was doing my hand embroidery, I had her join me in my crafts at home, and she chose to do cross-stitch. I felt like we were living in pioneer time, and we both enjoyed it so much! While doing crafts, she mentioned that the last time she did this craft was before she married my father. That meant when she was eighteen years old, over fifty-five years ago. I was so happy that she could go back to doing crafts and helping her relax. This was the result of God's work in me, and my mother was being blessed by my changes in life too. I had also stopped doing my craft around that same age too, and I had just gone back to it when God showed me in Germany about caring for my own needs. This craft helped me in Germany over the many nights when I could not sleep due to my trials. Doing my embroidery gave me much peace and allowed me to pray while I worked on it. It's amazing how God could use something so simple like doing "a craft" to bless and change your life and even the lives of others, like mothers.

Since my children were not little anymore, my youngest was now in middle school, and the other one was in high school. My stepson was living with us now. I felt led by the Lord to return full time to college. The homework and study time weren't easy as ten years had passed since I attended college. I did enjoy learning and especially doing the research but disliked writing the essays. I have never been a writer, so having to write ten or fifteen pages for an essay was hard, but I worked hard, and the Lord helped me through it. When I needed help with college, like having someone read some of my essays and have their input to make sure I was on the right track, my oldest son and even my youngest son helped. These boys were so young but so smart with words and writing, and both kept encouraging me about my college classes.

Soon the New Year arrived, and seven months had passed with us living in Missouri. I felt I no longer wanted to struggle with keeping my eyes on my broken marriage and its sorrows, but I wanted to fully keep my eyes on God. It was a Sunday service, and the pastor had just preached about the glory of God and finished with prayer. From my seat, I prayed. I asked God to take away my life of pain and instead give me joy and peace. I wanted to see his glory and bring Him glory. God answered my prayer, and I felt an immense joy that covered me and helped me put my eyes on Him. This gave me the courage and strength to remain focused on being a mother and stepmother, continuing full time in college and doing my ladies' home fellowship.

I kept my alone time to keep caring for my own needs, which included exercising, either walking in my neighborhood or at the gym, just like when I was in Germany. Months later we got orders to move again, so we only lived a year and a half in Missouri. We had to do the same thing again, saying goodbye to friends in the church and community. My husband was leaving soon to go overseas, and we were not allowed to go with him. I moved with my two sons back home to Oceanside, and my husband and stepson joined us a few days later.

California, July of 2013

We arrived back in California during the summer break, so my sons had enough time to get ready for the new school year. Our home was not ready for us to move in, so I had to stay in a hotel with my two sons and our dog. We stayed in a nearby county since the hotel was cheaper there than in our city of Oceanside. My husband arrived with my stepson, moved him back to live with his mother, and then moved in with us. So now it was four of us staying at the hotel, and we made the best of it.

But my husband and I lived as we lived before, separate lives. My husband stayed just a few weeks and then left for his new military job overseas. After few weeks of paying for the hotel, meals, and other expenses, I couldn't afford the stay. The military helped with the moving expenses but didn't cover it all since my waiting time was longer than what they usually covered.

So, I reached out to a good friend of mine who allowed us to stay at her house. We stayed with her probably for a month and then moved out once our home was ready. I was so blessed to have my friend. Her family accepted us into their homes, even with our dog, Gordo. They were so kind and patient with us and our dog. We moved into the home, and I worked on cleaning, painting, and making it our home again. My sons helped me unpack all our things except for my husband's personal stuff since he was overseas. We had to adjust to being back home again and living in a city, but we were happy to be living in our house and being part of our community again.

I attended my home church again with my two sons. I was blessed to see how the church had grown and was still teaching the message of Christ. There were so many new families that I did not know and so many good changes too. I reconnected with most of my friends from church and the neighborhood. Many asked if I was accepting donations and if I was going to be doing the mission work in Tijuana again, but my answer was no. One of the people who had asked me was a sister from church to whom I had donated a vehicle so she could help the family I had left to run the food ministry.

Before I had left for Germany, I had transferred my home food ministry to a family in Oceanside because no one could continue my mission work in Tijuana. I had left all the equipment with this family and trained them and this sister on how to help families in Oceanside and its surrounding areas. Now I was blessed to see that the food ministry I had started at home was not lost but continued. It is no longer at that family's home, but it has become a church ministry where it keeps helping families. I was happy to see that these servants of the Lord kept this food ministry running. I had visited and helped a few times in the food ministry and was so tempted to keep helping, but I did not because I knew that I was no longer able to do it but had to focus on my family and schooling.

I continued with my education at the same college, but now it was online instead of in class, although I would prefer to be sitting in a class instead of taking online classes. This was the only way I could finish my degree and still care for my family. My children continued their studies and enjoyed being home again, although we missed my husband, especially my kids. It was extremely hard being both parents, but God gave me the strength to do it while settling back in California. Then one day for the second time the Lord gave me Isaiah 60:1–2, "Arise, shine; for thy light is come, and the glory of the Lord is risen upon thee. For, behold, the darkness shall cover the earth, and gross darkness the people: but the Lord shall arise upon thee, and his glory shall be seen upon thee."

California, February of 2014

I knew that there was a reason why God was giving me this verse again, even though I could not understand it yet. Eight months later, February, I had to face the divorce petition. I needed to accept the fact that we had been living separate lives for more than five years and that the marriage was over. It was hard to face the reality because in my mind and heart I still desired to persist in having a wife relationship with him. We were still communicating but not realizing that it was mostly about the kids and the home. I was hoping that the distance would help us, but it did not. It just confirmed the reality of our lives that the marriage was over. In my heart, I was so broken. I knew of the pain that the divorce would cause my children and stepchildren. I could no longer avoid the truth: the marriage was over, and this would become my second divorce.

After facing this failure of my marriage, I just wanted to be alone and cry. All I wanted to do was to take refuge in the Lord, so I began reading and studying the Bible more than what I normally did and without the use of a concordance. Around a year after I arrived in Germany, I lost my Bible. This happened on a Sunday after church when I had taken my sons to eat lunch at a fast-food restaurant on the military base. On that day when I left the restaurant, I forgot my Bible. The next day I went to the restaurant but was told that it had been destroyed and I needed to speak to the military police since I had questions.

I could not understand why they would destroy a Bible. After that, I left for the military police station. After a few visits, I located the officer who handled the case. It was confirmed that it was destroyed. He told me that since it was an unattended black box left on the military base, they had to destroy it to ensure security. I was sad and told him what my Bible meant to me first because it was the Word of God and I had it for sixteen years. I received that Bible when I was pregnant with my first child and now regretted losing it. The Bible that was destroyed was a study one with concordance, study notes, maps, and much more, but I really didn't use it then since I did very little reading.

Since the loss of that Bible, much has changed. Now I have a bilingual Bible, English and Spanish, with no concordance or study notes, but this has helped me so much for my spiritual growth. I would constantly find myself seeking God and being more captivated by Him, wanting to know more about him, the Bible, and Israel. One day I felt prompted by the Lord to fast. I think this was a result of me seeking Him. So, I fasted because I needed his strength because I was about to go through a legal divorce. Just the thought of having to fill out forms and go through the court process was causing me stress, but I needed to face it. Also, I was fasting because I wanted to know the Lord's will and needed his provision and direction for my life and for my children's life. So, in April of 2014, I fasted for five days during the Easter week. God would answer my prayers, and I would get to experience God intimately like I had never known before in my life!

Five Days of Fasting and Prayer

California, April of 2014, Easter Week

The Cross

It is Thursday, my second day of fasting. I went for a walk, and when I looked at the skies, I saw a drawing in the clouds. My first thought was how romantic it was, but then right away I felt led to pray. I said, "Lord, I am alone, and I have no husband, so that drawing can't be my life. I am going through my second divorce."

God then said to me, "Divorce yourself."

Since I did not understand the meaning, I asked, "What do you mean? I am going through my divorce. What do you mean?"

He answered, "This is what I mean, Delilah. Divorce yourself from yourself and go to the Cross to be One with Me." He was asking me to come to the Cross and meet Him there so I could be married to Him. He was asking me to die to myself and come to Him at the Cross.

You can see the drawing below. The drawing has two heads and one body. The body and head are Jesus with his big heart, and only the other head represents me, Delilah. Jesus Christ and I are walking together, crucified with Him. This is the marriage he wants me to have, and only at the cross is where I can be One with Jesus.

God gave me these two verses along with this vision:

"For no man ever yet hated his own flesh; but nourisheth and cherisheth it, even as the Lord the church" (Ephesians 5:29).

"Then said Jesus unto his disciples, If any man will come after me, let him deny himself, and take up his cross, and follow me" (Matthew 16:24).

For no man ever yet hated his own flesh; but nourisheth and cherisheth it, even as the LORD the church: Eph 5:29
Porque nadie aborreció jamás a su propia carne, sino que la sustenta y la cuida, como también Cristo a la iglesia, Efe 5:29

Si alguno quiere venir en pos de mí, niéguese a sí mismo, y tome su cruz, y sígueme. Mat 16:24
If any man will come after me, let him deny himself, and take up his cross, and follow me. Matt 16:24

38

On this same day, I visited a friend for two consecutive days, and while visiting, I shared with her my first vision I had in Germany about the heart and this one, the cross. I shared how happy I was to hear God speak to me and how each vision had blessed me. Also, I told her that I did not understand what I was supposed to do with these visions and that this whole experience was something new to me.

She was blessed by the two visions I shared and told me that she believed that God was giving me a book to write. She then told me that it would be a blessing for others to hear God's revelations given to me. I was blessed by her response, but I was having a hard time seeing myself as a writer, much less an author, but did receive what she said to me.

During my visit, we prayed and fellowshipped, and her son joined us too. I felt so blessed to have them in my life, people with whom I could speak deeply about the Lord and pray with. On that day, I walked back home very blessed because she understood that God was speaking to me and of the method that he was using.

The Dream

It is Good Friday and my third day of fasting. I dreamed that I was sitting down in a small chair that fit only one person. My head was bent over because I was writing on a small brown table that was a little long on the sides. This table had enough space for me to write on my paper and with enough elbow space on the side for my writing materials, pencils, and pens. I saw that somebody was standing behind me, and he was dictating to me what to write. I saw myself writing obediently what this person was dictating. At no point in my dream did I turn my face, but I was completely focused on writing what the person behind me was telling me. I did not see his face, just his radiant eyes and that he was dressed all in white.

I saw clearly that I was sitting with my head down and my hand was writing what he told me to write. I kept writing and writing, and I knew that nothing was coming from my mind, but it was from the person dressed in white. I was only his writer. And this was how my dream ended.

The Vision

It is Saturday, my fourth day of fasting. I received this revelation through a vision. I got on my knees to pray and thank God for everything He revealed and because I would finish my fast the next day at noon. I prayed with my eyes closed, and at the end of my prayer, God gave me a vision.

God told me, "Delilah, as I passed over you and covered you with my wings, this is what I leave you as a reminder that I have been with you. I leave you this book; your book is complete." And He showed me the number seven, and that is how my vision ended. I knew God said my book was complete, but at this time, I had no idea of what He meant by this.

Arise, shine; for thy light is come, and the glory of the Lord is risen upon thee. For, behold, the darkness shall cover the earth, and gross darkness the people: but the Lord shall arise upon thee, and his glory shall be seen upon thee.
—Isaiah 60:1-32

Delilah P.I.O.

This month was amazing because of the new revelations that came from the five-day fast, but also it was a tough month. This was the hardest time for my children and me because I had to face more than just the divorce. I was in financial need due to my divorce and hit with much sickness too. My oldest son, Gershom, was a senior in high school and desired to visit his dream college.

At the beginning of the year, I had saved money and purchased two plane tickets for him and me to visit his dream school, Penn State University, where he wanted to attend. Unfortunately, two days before this trip I was diagnosed with influenza, which prevented me from traveling and accompanying him. It was not only this. I had no spending money to give him for this trip; nor did I have money to provide for us at home. My financial need was so great that Gershom would give me some of his spending money that he received from his father so we could buy food at a dollar store. I kept my finances to myself and my kids, but some of our friends, our neighbors, helped us. They were not aware of my financial need, but they did know I was facing divorce, so that was what showed them our needs.

I was as vulnerable and in need as all those families I had served and helped for so many years. It was very painful and hard to believe what was happening to me. I had nothing to give, but I had so many needs. The good thing was that now I knew to ask for help for me and to receive when in need. I asked for help from the food ministry at my church, and they graciously met my needs.

In the middle of the week, I felt I no longer could go on since I was so sick. I had high fevers, lots of body aches, trouble breathing at night so I could not sleep, and so much weakness. I could not stop being a mother. How could I do that? I also had to continue with my classes, and I had to be strong and recover soon because my sons needed me, but I also needed someone to care for me.

Around the third day of being sick and seeing what I was against, I felt I could no longer go through with my life. I felt like I was dying and fainting, but God would sustain me. On that day, I reached out to my oldest son's father, and he was able to help me financially with some money. Then this same day my brother, the pastor, called me. He had no idea of what I was going through. He put my younger nephew on the phone, and both prayed for me. Although I was still extremely sick and broken, this call made me feel very loved.

After hanging up the phone, I felt I had nothing left in me to give and keep going because of how sick and weak I was. I was so broken. How could I move on with my life if I was so empty? How could I care for my own children if I had nothing to give them? I could not provide for them when I was so broken.

This is when I heard the voice of God saying to me, "Delilah, remember from where I brought you and where you are today. Remember where you were born and look where you are today and how far you have come."

This made me think of the place where I was born and every country and place, I had been. It made me see how I was still alive despite all the difficulties in my life. Who would have thought that this little child born in a Third World country and to a large family of twelve brothers and sisters, with her being number eleven and the youngest girl, would live and get to travel to many parts of the world? Who would have thought that she would get to live in America and get to help families in Mexico and America?

After reflecting on what God showed me, I said to Him, "God, I see how far you have brought me, and today I accept these sufferings in my life even though they are exceedingly difficult and painful, but I accept them. Help me to press on. I'm going to trust you no matter what happens in my life."

And immediately I played a worship song, which I made into a prayer for the first time in my life. On this day, I agreed to do God's will and not mine. I agreed to receive with a good attitude the bad things and sufferings in my life, not just the good things. Thank God who protected my sons because none of them got sick, and neither did the friends who brought me food by my door.

Even though my children saw my husband and me living separate lives for few years, it was still hard for them to know that we were no longer a family, and the divorce was happening. I could not avoid the pain that the divorce caused our children, but what I could do was be strong so I could help my sons. They were young teenagers and barely adapting to being back home and in a new school, and now they had to face the divorce. They were ending the high school year. The youngest was in his first year, and the eldest was in his senior year. These were big changes for them, apart from all the things they had to face like any young men at their age. It was also sad to see my stepchildren suffer and live separate lives from us. I continued with my studies because I was determined to finish my career no matter what was happening in my life.

The school year ended, and Gershom was preparing to go away for college. This was a happy moment for him and for me as a mother. Financially I was without the resources to send him to college, but I trusted God, our provider. The month of August came, and Gershom went to live and study at his dream university, which was on the other side of the country. I stayed home with my son, Moses, and went through exceedingly difficult times with him because of the divorce and his young age, as he was only fourteen when this happened.

It was the beginning of November. I had just finished my Bible study time and prayed when God made me see that this study applied to my life and not just to others.

He also gave me Isaiah 61:1–3, "The Spirit of the Lord God is upon me; because the Lord hath anointed me to preach good tidings unto the meek; He hath sent me to bind up the brokenhearted, to proclaim liberty to the captives, and the opening of the prison to them that are bound; To proclaim the acceptable year of the Lord, and the day of vengeance of our God; to comfort all that mourn; To appoint unto them that mourn in Zion, to give unto them beauty for ashes, the oil of joy for mourning, the garment of praise for the spirit of heaviness; that they might be called trees of righteousness, the planting of the Lord, that He might be glorified."

Then He said to me, "Delilah, you have been walking with me for twenty-five years since you came back after you had walked away when you were nineteen years old. You are doing good now, and this is not about a current sin. I know how much you love and desire me, but you need to know that you rebelled against me when you walked away from my ways at the age of nineteen. You accepted me at the altar call as your Savior at the age of twelve and the age of sixteen accepted your calling."

When God said this to me, I had a flashback. I was able to see myself at those two altar calls. And how much I had forgotten about those days! especially the one on my calling. It was like if I was watching a video. This is what I did when I walked back to the Lord. I never asked him to forgive me but walked back with him like I had done nothing wrong. God showed me this not because he hadn't forgiven me. He did. But it was for me to see that I had done wrong by abandoning God and that I was still struggling with this. I needed to be delivered from the stronghold of being rebellious against God. In response, I asked God to forgive me for my rebellious and prideful heart. I cried for so many days, but my tears were those of joy.

During that same week, I asked my two ex-husbands and their children to forgive me for the pain I had caused in their lives. God delivered me on that day from being rebellious and prideful. I did not realize before how much pride and rebellious attitude I had toward God and people too. This forgiveness and deliverance made me feel free for the first time in my life and made me feel that I was a lady and not just a woman. I believed, so I felt for the first time that I was a woman of worth! I felt as if I were a young lady of nineteen years of age again and that God had saved all the desires of my heart and I could live the life he had planned for me to live. I finally belonged all to God, and nothing was in the way of having a great relationship with him. On that day, Romans 8:28 came to my mind, "And we know that all things work together for good to them that love God, to them who are the called according to his purpose."

On this day, for the first time in my life, I felt worthy to be desired by any godly man to become his wife. That is why I was able to pray and write this in my diary, which is in the prologue of this book, "No man can satisfy me until I am satisfied with My Great I AM, Jesus! If God has a missionary husband for me, He will provide it, and if not, I accept my singleness." This day I felt that I could prioritize focusing on God and that He would bring a Christian man into my life if it were his will.

Seeking Guidance

My encounters with God kept happening. He kept giving me more to write, and for many days and nights, I was restless because God would be speaking to me, and I would become overwhelmed by how much He would reveal to me. I had no idea what was happening to me. I kept praying about what to do with the writings. They were a blessing to me, and I was feeling that I needed to share it with others as my friend suggested but did not know how though. I sought direction from a leader at my church and set a meeting, at which I shared with her what was happening, that God had confronted me about when I had walked away from Him and showed me about my strongholds and given me understanding about it. I shared how I was experiencing for the first time in my life God's revelations through visions, dreams, and writings. And He had shown me through a vision how I was to minister when the time came to share all his revelations, but I did not know where I was supposed to do it. So, I was seeking to find out if I were to share my writings here at our home church or if I were to do it in Mexico. I told her that I had done a few small women's conferences, but they were based on testimonials or a book, something quite different from what I had now.

This time I was having teachings that God was giving me to write, and I needed to know how to go about sharing them. I was seeing that I needed to share them in the United States because my writings had been bilingual, English and Spanish. Those were the two languages I was fluent in.

I shared with the leader what I was going through in my personal life, the divorce. This leader gave me her input about what I shared. In regards to strongholds, she had told me that if I were to share here at the church, I could not bring in the subject of strongholds because this would create confusion among the believers. She said that a believer cannot have strongholds because Christ had already set that person free. I completely agreed with her that Christ had set us free but shared how God showed me how I still had strongholds, and I gave her an example of one and how it had entered my life.

We could not agree, so I had to just let it go. Her answer so puzzled me, but I thanked her for seeing me. This leader said I could not minister the way I was told since we did not do that at our church. God had shown me a vision of me ministering in a crowd through speaking, praying, and visiting homes of those who allowed me and praying for them and that I was joined by my team. But I was told I could not do that here because our church did not operate that way.

So, I shared with her that I had a ministry like that in Tijuana, and I did it with my brother, a pastor. We visited homes and brought food to those in need. We prayed for healing, simply fellowshipped, or gave encouragement and always prayed for them before we left their home or ministry. To be a help to them while on the battlefield. But I was being told that we didn't do this in America, and I never knew that there would be a difference in how you reached out and prayed for families. Mexican, American, or any culture, they all have a need. And I would think they would all want someone to visit them and show how important they are and that in their time of need, someone was here for them with a word of encouragement and prayer.

I was shocked that this was something you didn't do in the United States because I had done this for my neighbors, friends, and some of the families I had distributed food to. It was always a blessing to do it, and it always brought me closer to God and people and made me aware of their needs and existence. This is what makes me be part of the body of Christ. Jesus visited homes and places and did not just minister at the temple, so we are to do the same when needed. I understood that she was not called to do this ministry, but that does not mean that she should say that this type of ministry is not something that we don't do here in our church in America.

I respected her answer and told her I understood the culture, and I left it at that. She then told me that she was happy that God was speaking to me and prayed that he would show me how to serve him, and that was how the meeting ended. I knew I would keep serving the way God had shown me. No matter in which country or place I am, I will keep seeking to serve as Jesus did. This leader could not help me, and I left confused by her answers but not discouraged because I knew in my heart and spirit that God was being real in my life, just like his revelations.

God showed me through this experience to not depend on man but to be fully dependent on him. Why? Because a leader may not be able to help, and this may get me discouraged and stop me from seeking him. So, I needed to keep pursuing God because he would reveal his plans and calling for my life, only by remaining focused on him. Also, this experience was to remind me to be a good leader and of the need to have good leaders in the church, the body of Christ, and its responsibilities.

We are to have well-prepared leaders who can direct the flock of God, and if as a leader we cannot or are not willing to direct the flock, then we need to remove ourselves from that privileged position and allow those who have the calling and heart to do it. I know that there are cases where a leader may not understand what that person is going through because they have not experienced it, but they can pray for direction on how to help. There may be times where their only help is to pray and then connect them with someone who has gone through that process or may have the same calling.

I understand that leaders are humans, and oftentimes they can be so busy with ministry, their personal life, and trials that they may not seek God on how to help those when they come seeking direction. It is imperative that as leaders, we be aware when the Holy Spirit is working in someone's life and brings them into our lives to come alongside them in prayer or direction or as a mentor. This experience helped me to remain focused only on God so I could know what to do with my life and writings. And God reminded me that this is His church and that He died for her. He also reminded me of how precious the body of Christ, the church, is to Him, so I needed to keep praying for her.

I spent so many years trying to get rid of my anxiety and colon problems but with no success. No matter how healthy I ate, nothing worked, but then after twenty years of sickness, I was no longer having this problem. I had attributed my healing to my new life as a single woman because my divorce was final at the beginning of December. So, I was no longer being stressed by marriage problems, but God showed me I was wrong. He showed me that this sickness was a heavy stronghold that entered so long ago into my life, but when I repented from being rebellious and prideful and restored my relationship with Him, that is how my healing happened!

When God showed me this, it made me think of the woman mentioned in the Bible who was sick for five years with bleeding but was healed just by touching Jesus. I was just like her now. I was free from sickness! I was no longer depending on sugary products to calm me. When I would start feeling anxious, I would go to God and try to do it right away with my worries, and by doing so, I had his peace. I still ate sweet stuff, but it was no longer an addiction. I would eat it in moderate portions as a treat. I still watched my diet, but I no longer had to drink products to have a normally functioning colon.

There were other changes I had to face and were not as good as my health, but I had to face them. It was hard to be back home and having the people at church or the community ask where my husband was. To avoid giving explanations, I simply told them that he was overseas for work without disclosing my marital status, and only my close friends knew about my divorce. At church, I could not stop other people from finding out though. A few criticized me because of my new marital status, and they let me know in a very cruel way. They had no idea how much they hurt me and how they made me feel rejected and judged. I was not strong enough to continue going to the same church and see those people who criticized me. I was away for over three years and so happy to be back at my home church but being treated this way really hurt me.

Their criticism made me feel that I was not worthy of God's calling for my life. So, I decided it was best to leave my home church and attend another Christian church. I longed so much to continue serving God, but how could I do it if I felt that people only saw me as a divorced missionary who had failed God? In this new church, I was able to focus on my healing and continue to grow spiritually while I was adapting to my life as a single mother again.

Soon after my divorce, a man from my home church called me and invited me for coffee, and I accepted his invitation. Both of us were single, and I never thought that something could happen between us. I was newly divorced, and he was a new widower. I kept many families in my intercessory prayers, and his was one of them. I did not know much about him except that he had been attending my home church for many years and I had seen him serving. I did not know anything about his life, but I just knew him as one of the many families in my church who had supported my mission work in Tijuana with donations and joined us on mission trips. It was not uncommon for him to have my phone number, as every person who gave donations had it. It was strange to receive his invitation though, but I accepted because I thought I could use a break from everything that was going on in my life and instead get some fellowship.

We went out and enjoyed our talk. I agreed to go out with him again, and I never thought anything else would come out of these coffee trips. I would share with him about the transformation that God was doing in my life. We each talked about what we were planning to do with our lives, what the future would look like. We never thought we would fall in love, but it happened. Soon we fell in love, but before I agreed to be his girlfriend, I had to seek God.

I was full of fear about this new relationship and worried because of my divorce and the pains that it brought me. There was one evening when I was praying about this new relationship, and I felt God telling me not to fear but showed me what to do. I obeyed and had peace about it, and I did as he instructed me. I opened my heart to this man with honesty and shared how I was feeling and what I been through. I shared how much I needed to be loved, and if he were willing to accept me as I was with my past and love on me, then we could try our relationship, but if he couldn't, it was better not to try it at all.

He told me he wanted to date me, so I agreed for him to be the man I longed to have. In the short time we went out, I noticed good qualities in him, which I longed to have in the man I would fall in love with since I was a young adult. I was happy to be dating him and proud of our relationship and that he was serving God through the church.

I did not know how this dating was going to go, and I did not even know how to tell my kids about it. The last time I dated was over thirteen years ago, which was my ex-husband. My sons accepted our relationship and were happy for us. I started to date, but I continued attending my church until one day I joined my boyfriend at an event at my old church. Right after this, I decided to go back. He was happy that we were attending the same church, and I was happy too. I had missed being part of the church that I had belonged to for over eleven years and where I had many friends. It was awkward to be attending my home church after I was known as a married missionary before, but now I was single and dating. Now I was being seen with a different man, whom many people knew too and was also a recent widower. I was judged before for being divorced, and now I was judged for dating and for whom I was dating. I was not strong enough to withstand criticism from some people but allowed it to affect me many times, making me cry over all the bad things I was accused of.

With prayers and my boyfriend's support, we were able to overcome the criticism, and I had to learn to build a "thick skin," as they say in English. God showed me that the attacks were from the enemy and that I needed to rebuke all the lies said about me and not to believe or entertain them. I had to pray for my children to be protected from hearing those lies. I had to learn to not hold it against those who criticized me but forgive them, just like Jesus, and pray that God would open their eyes to see the truth and get to know me for who I really was.

I enjoyed getting to know my boyfriend when he joined me on a missionary trip. I had made a Christmas banquet for seven pastors and their families in Tijuana. At this event, we served a great dinner, gave them many gifts, and prayed for each of them and their families. It was so beautiful to share all this with my boyfriend. It was a good way to start our courtship. Praying and serving together was so nice that I could see his giving and serving heart.

A month passed, and now I needed to move but was not prepared. I was given short notice and not ready to face all the challenges it brought to my life. I was a single mother responsible for my son at college and my teenage son at home. I was still taking college classes, focused on packing everything to move out with my youngest and our dog. There was no help for this move, but I had to do it alone with my youngest son. We had to separate my stuff from my ex-husband's, and this was just too much to deal with. I was also in my new love relationship too, and we were starting to have some issues due to his anger problem. I did not pay much attention because I felt it was normal because he was still grieving and his recent life changes, and I felt he soon would get over it.

My problems and life situation hit me faster than I could process it. Not seeing the situation that my boyfriend was in because he had so much going on in his life, I asked him for help. I did not know what else to do. I asked if we could move in with him and said I would contribute to the house expenses, and so we did. I moved into one room and my son into another room, and I brought only our personal things and put our larger belongings in storage. Unfortunately moving together with my boyfriend was not a good idea because we had fallen into temptation and soon after living in the same house we began living together like a couple.

I would have so much remorse for what we had done. This relationship was so special to me, and I did not want to live in sin. I thought I was strong, and it would not happen since I was walking closer to God, but it did happen. We both repented and committed to not live in sin, but they were times we failed. So, he had to step down from serving at church because of the sin. On the other hand, I was no longer doing mission work because I was focused on my school and family. We were in love and desired to marry, so we got engaged, and months later we married.

I saw a friend from church months later. We got to spend some time together while I took her on a trip to Tijuana to visit her family. On that trip, I got to know her better. I shared with her about the hardships I went through when my children were little. This friend was impressed with my story and how I had overcome it all. She suggested I should write my story and publish it in a book. The following time I saw her at church, she asked if I was working on my book, as she had given me a program to help me write. I told her I was not writing at all but desired to write a missionary book one day, but just did not believe I could be a writer.

She was not the first person to tell me that I should write my story of when my children were little. My family and close friends had suggested the same. I did desire to write that story but felt I could not do it yet because I was not ready to share it. I lost contact with my friend, but sometimes I would think of her and her suggestion about becoming a writer.

The Sign

A year and a half had passed since I had my last vision. I had been married now for six months and had already finished my degree, but I made plans that I would wait to look for work in that field. It was important for me to stay focused on helping my son and be available for his last two years of high school so he could be ready for college. I focused on taking care of my home and being a good wife and mother. I was not sure about how to go about using my degree to get a job in the future. When the time came, I would then worry about that. I continued spending time with God and still desired to write my missionary book but felt the need for more confirmation from God on becoming a writer.

My marriage was not doing so well, which discouraged me from even considering writing a book. Many months went by, and at the beginning of the new year, I asked God to give me a sign. I was very specific about which sign to give me. I asked the Lord to enable me to locate the home of my first pastor in Campeche. I wanted to get a remembrance of my pastor, a photo, and get more information about his life since I would need it if I was to write a missionary book. I wanted to write about him in that missionary book. He was my inspiration. I was aware that this pastor had died many years ago, but I knew that his family still lived in Campeche.

So, in January of 2016, I visited Campeche with my husband, and one day we went to look for the pastor's home. After much walking, I was able to locate it. I had the opportunity to talk with one of his daughters, and she had a vague memory of who I was. I then shared with her about desiring to write a missionary book. I desired to have a photo of her father, my pastor. He was such a great spiritual influence in my life and a great example of a humble man, full of love and obedience to God. I shared with her how I remembered that he would be preaching to us in Spanish, but on some occasions, he would say some words in the Mayan language too. After talking for a while, she asked me to come back in the evening after she had gotten help in locating the box that contained her family memories.

Once the evening came, I returned to the pastor's home, accompanied by my husband, and this time we drove instead of walking. Campeche's climate is extremely hot and humid, and the house was probably like a twenty-minute walk. So, we did not want to risk not making it all the way due to the heat. My husband waited in the car while I went inside the house since we thought this would be a quick visit because I was just picking up a photo.

I had no idea of what was waiting for me inside of that home. My pastor's daughter greeted me, and she then proceeded to show me some photos and a Bible, my pastor's Bible. I instantly recognized the Bible without being told. I could remember when the pastor used to carry it and used it to preach. I opened the Bible and asked if I could take pictures of the Bible and the photos that were inside.

His daughter then said to me, "My father left two Bibles, and I am giving you this one. I think that my father would be very happy to know that you have it and that you are still serving God."

I insisted that I couldn't take it, but she made me see that it would be a blessing if I were to receive it, as this would be a great way to honor her father, knowing that a servant of God had it. She reminded me that she had a second Bible that her father left and that she knew how much I would value this Bible.

I was speechless. I thanked her from the bottom of my heart for the privilege of receiving something so precious, the Bible of my first pastor, Brother Canito. I then knew that this was God's answer to my prayer, and it was more than what I asked for. This was a sign of God. He was telling me to believe Him and obey Him.

So, after I said goodbye to her, I got in the car, where my husband was patiently waiting. I was crying and speechless, and that is not me. I am never speechless. All I could do was just show my husband the Bible, and when I was done crying, I spoke. I had shared with my husband before we planned this trip of what I prayed for, so now my husband was witnessing God's answer to my prayer. We both were in awe of what had just happened, that God had just confirmed that I needed to dedicate myself to writing.

My Burdens

It was the month of February, and God would bring another change in my life. I was struggling with the idea of being a writer and being used by God because of certain feelings and issues I was still having. The change happened in me by asking for help. I set up a counseling appointment with my younger brother, the pastor who lived in Tijuana. I knew I could no longer carry my shame, pain, regrets, and being tormented again by horrible thoughts like I had in the past. I drove alone to Tijuana, and minutes before I crossed the border and lost radio signal, I got to hear in a Christian radio station, a short testimony of a person who overcame being constantly tormented by his thoughts. (This was divine appointment and not coincidence.)

This testimony encouraged me to be transparent once I met with my brother. This brother has also been my partner in ministry, and I could not think of anyone better to help me but my brother. I shared with him for the first time in my life my painful thoughts that had tormented me many times in my life. I did not go into details since I did not think it was necessary, but I focused on just sharing why I had suffered and how I was still suffering. I needed him to hear me as a pastor and not just as my brother, and he did. He had seen me suffer but did not know what burdens I had been carrying with me. He prayed for me and gave me instructions on how to pray alone at home, to anoint my head and rededicate my life and whole body to the Lord.

I had always asked God to change my thoughts, but I had never done this type of prayer. I returned home, and alone in a room, I anointed my head and prayed, asking God to forgive me for committing fornication and any unconfessed sin. Then I prayed, rejecting every evil thing I had brought into my life and what others had brought into my life. I then rededicated my whole being to God from my head to my toes.

As I was praying, I finally could see how God saw me, that I was pure for Him because I am his daughter, and everything is in the past. This prayer brought me freedom from chains, shame, and feelings of worthlessness and guilt, and this rededication put me in the place that God had for me as his daughter. Finally, I could live free of all the things that tormented me since my childhood and live free of shame. Thank God for his forgiveness and love and for seeing me of worth and giving me an abundant life! Thank God for my brother too! After this, I felt invigorated with a stronger faith in God. I felt more focused on how to go about doing what He wanted me to do using the education I had and with the writings He had given me.

Hidden Sins

May of 2016

It was good to be growing in the Word and having a closer relationship with God, but I could not say the same thing for my husband and me because our relationship was not getting to be so good. We were having some real problems and not much communication, so the issues were never dealt with. It seemed as if he could not deal with it, but instead he would just shut down or leave me after he would get so angry. And upon his return, which would be a few days later, things would not be dealt with, but were all dismissed as it never happened. When I tried to bring it up, he would just ask me to let it go and move on, and if I insisted, things would escalate into a fight.

So, to keep the peace, I would just have to let go, but this was destroying our relationship and me. His abandonment started to affect me that I would let my imagination fly away. I was constantly tempted to pursue my desire that I had before we dated, to move back to Mexico. He was not willing to talk, to fix the marriage, and on top of that, he would leave me. What else was I supposed to do? I was feeling not wanted, and his behavior showed me that the marriage was not important to him because if it were, he would work with me to make it better and do counseling, if that were what would help us, but this was not happening.

This was hard to believe. I was in another broken marriage, and what would I do now? Do I give into my plans, or what else could I do? I felt led by the Lord to examine what I possess, and I read Exodus 20:17, "Thou shalt not covet thy neighbour's house, thou shalt not covet thy neighbour's wife, nor his manservant, nor his maidservant, nor his ox, nor his ass, nor any thing that is thy neighbour's. Then I wrote what the Lord showed me on that day."

What do I have that God could use for his glory? The answer: Tangible and non-tangible things. Which things?

- **Tangible:** Car, computer, TV, cell phone, cooking dishes and kitchen appliances, books, furniture, and exercise equipment
- **Non-tangible:** The need to possess the United States, knowledge of the Bible, testimonies, marriage, bilingual, degree, cooking, talking, teaching, helping, study, learning, and time

God will use this to supply my needs and of others. Do I possess the tangible and non-tangible things I have? I have struggled with the idea of wanting to be somewhere else instead of living in America, and this only happens every time I have arguments with my husband. My first reaction after I am getting abandoned was to flee to Mexico and do what I had planned to do before I married him. I also wanted to leave because I missed home too. Why should I remain here when I was constantly mistreated and not wanted? Before I married him, I planned to move back home once my youngest son graduated from high school and open a ministry in Mexico, but instead I married so I had to say goodbye to those plans.

Christ was rejected because the Israelites did not see him as theirs, but they looked for someone else, even though he was physically there. They could see Jesus; they could welcome him and accept him and all his blessings, but most of them did not.

I Delilah, I am desiring, coveting others' lives, while God has given me the best, but because my eyes are on another country and other people, I cannot see and accept my possessions, my blessings. This is because of the way I am living with my husband in constant discontent and pain. This is also because I feel alone and miss home so much and keep comparing my life back home to my current life, and I have struggled with this for a few years but did not realize the wrong of it until now.

So, I said to God, "I ask that you forgive me for coveting other people's lives. I recognize that I have sinned against you and how this has affected me that I could not fully enjoy the blessing of living in the United States." This was a hidden sin covered with the fact that I felt it was normal to miss home but did not realize that I was sinning. I was desiring to have their lives and not accepting mine. That I was married and that my place is to be with my husband despite all our difficulties. Lord, you put me in the lives of the people from Mexico to help them, but I am not to covet their lives. In Jesus's name, I pray this. Amen."

More questions arise. Who am I? Is it God's will for me to live in the United States, or is it my own will? What happened to me the last time I lived in Mexico? My plans failed! From birth and until now, God had allowed me to live in different countries. Why? Do they have a part in my calling? What is really my calling?

I see my list of the tangible and non-tangible things that I possess, and I ask myself, "What do I really possess? Do I even possess the United States, a country where I have put my roots and that I love? Do I own or live on borrowed land, memories, and other people's dreams? Why do I live like this? Is this from God?"

I answered myself and said, "The answer is no! This is not from God! God has plans for me, Delilah, so I do not need to desire, want, or covet what He has for others in Mexico or somewhere else. I accept the country of the United States as fully my country, as my place of living, no matter what is going on in my marriage or life, and I thank you for this country, Lord, and all the other countries you have blessed me to live in. I now must possess all the other things I have on my list." God has specifically designed and written plans for me, Delilah. What are those plans? The only way for me to know it is by seeking the Master King Jesus and asking Him, and He will speak to me. He will write to me and give me his guidance. He will show me and tell me how to live the plans God has for me. But I need to submit my will, life, and wants and no longer have memories of where I was born and wishing I could live that same way. And I need to stop coveting those who live back home, but I need to be content and accept my life here in the United States as it is. I can miss home and the people, but I need to make sure not to fall into coveting, into desiring, to have their lives. I now need to start by looking and moving forward to the life Delilah has and needs to live in God's will, purpose, and provision. My obedience to God will provide my purpose in life!

A Young Man

A family reached out to me because they needed help in making school decisions for their young adult son. I had the opportunity to help this young man and his parents in making a good decision about his school and future. After I helped them, I felt led by God to write material on how to help a young person and their parents. God opened the door, and I was able to use this material to give a free workshop at the church where my brother pastors in Tijuana. This helped me see why many years ago God told me to go back to school and finish my degree. I was able to see how what I studied, which is science in human services.

God has used it to help me recognize my own traumas and be more prepared to help others. Now I did not just have my twenty years of missionary work experience, but now I have academic schooling too. I decided to study human services because this degree was the closest to missionary work and I wanted to use it to become a speaker and mentor to keep helping families. At the time when I decided what degree to study, I had no idea of writing a book, much less knowing what God was planning for my life. Giving this workshop motivated me to see myself working as a speaker and mentor.

The School

Now the month of June is here, and I am battling between hearing God and hearing my life problems that this marriage presents, more arguments and disagreements. My husband knew I been a missionary for a long time but struggled on accepting that I still wanted to serve God now that we were married. When we dated, we talked about my calling and career and how I planned to keep serving God since the marriage should not change anything, especially now that I had no little children to raise. I love being a wife and knew it was my first ministry, but I also knew that God had a purpose for me besides being a wife and mother. And when it comes to work, I was desiring to get a job where I could help people.

Every time I tried to share with my husband my encounters with God, my writings, and the type of work I wanted to do, he would refuse to listen and accept it. His reaction and negativity would make me incredibly sad and feel isolated, so I had to just keep it to myself. The only thing left to do was to pray for him and our marriage. My husband had accepted for me to write my missionary book since he saw God's confirmation for it, but he was not seeing it as a job and disapproved of me becoming a speaker and mentor. I persisted in seeking God's will because I needed to know that I was not imagining this change in my life and that I was doing the right thing despite my husband's lack of understanding and interest.

Now I needed to know which step to take next, so on my birthday, I visited a Christian seminary school, thinking that maybe I needed to enroll so I could become a speaker and writer. I thought maybe I could drive to school every day and then come back home every day instead of living in the dorms. Maybe I could go to school while my husband was working and my son was at school for his senior year. Once I got home, I shared with my husband about my visit to the seminary and my thoughts about God using me as a speaker and writer.

I instantly saw how his face changed and seemed very worried so much that he refused to hear more about it, so I had to just let it go. I had to just keep praying and seeking God. I looked for another school on the internet. I was looking at which options I had and what would be best for me. I was making plans to visit it when I heard the voice of God telling me, "Delilah, do not sign up because if you do so, you will be busy with school and at home, and you won't have time for me. Continue seeking me and spending time with me. You are already in school! You are in my school!"

I accepted his answer and did not enroll in any human seminary school, but I continued in God's seminary. I kept spending time alone with Him, walking and growing in his Word. God was teaching me and would continue teaching me!

Alone with God

Five days after my birthday, I wrote this prayer to the Lord.

> A prisoner in the Lord, I, Delilah, as a prisoner of the Lord, I am in his time and will. I have no authority to command or say what I should do, but God is the one who tells me what to do and how to do it. And the only day I will leave this prison of God will be to meet him face-to-face; meanwhile God keeps me between his four walls for my own good and his glory. In these four walls, I do not lack anything, and no one distracts me. Just as a prisoner is only released in fulfilling his sentence, so God will release me when I have served my sentence, which is to fulfill my purpose for which I was created and for which I was born. When God releases me from prison, it will be for me to come before his presence, like in the court when the person appears before the judge. For I will stand before God when my work here on earth is done, and I, Delilah, will come face-to-face with my judge, my Creator, my great I AM, and He will say to me, "Delilah, Good work! You have been faithful, my servant. Come to rest in my presence." Meantime I am still on this earth, and I continue to be inside the prison (the hands of God, the will of God), imprisoned where I cannot escape these four walls because I want to be sure that I do his will, that my needs are met, and that I bring Him glory. I do not want to make mistakes anymore; I do not want to be a woman with no direction and no purpose anymore! I want to remain imprisoned in God's prison (in his hands, in his will), and this is the only way I, Delilah, want to live! Yes, God, help me. Guide me to stand and remain

in your four walls as your prisoner and satisfied in your will. I need you to guide me and that I may feel your love always. Thank you for choosing me to be with you and to be your prisoner, Jesus Christ, and it is in the name of Jesus that I ask this prayer. Thank you. Amen!

My freedom will be when I meet you face-to-face! I'm isolated from the world to be Jesus's prisoner!

Your servant and prisoner,
Delilah

Yes, You!

July 2016

It was now July, and I would have another encounter with God, another vision. The book cover is the picture of this vision, my encounter with God. In this picture, you see a crowd and a hand. I am the one in the middle of the crowd with the pink, fuchsia dress. The hand is God's hand calling me, but I am thinking that He is calling someone else in the crowd and not me. My finger is pointing to my face because I am questioning God, saying, "You are calling me? You want me to do this? Are you sure? Why me? If you can find great godly women out there who have been married just one time and have not had struggles like me, they should be used for sharing their life story and not me! Plus, I am not a writer but a talker. There is no way I could write! And you want me to write in two languages, Spanish and English? That is even harder! No, I cannot! Plus, I only speak plain Spanish and English, and I do not have the education to do this. Furthermore, if I were to share my life story, it would be a bad testimony instead of a good one." This would be said, 'This is what you don't do in your life instead of this is what you do in your life' because I would write it with transparency, and they would be able to see all my faults! Well, this would cause people to make fun of you, God, and point fingers at me because of what a bad example I am of a godly woman."

Oh, but God was not calling anyone else in the crowd but me, Delilah. And so, He said to me, "Yes, you!" So, God wanting to use my life story to bring Him glory was something impossible for me to believe!

Finally, my answer to God was, "Yes, God, I will write the book, but the missionary book I had in mind, not my life story."

And this is how this vision ended.

63

David, the King

I was struggling with shame and still had the thoughts that I would receive bad criticism once people read my life story. God then encouraged me to look in the Bible at the life of Abraham, Samson, and then David, and David was the one who was the strongest in helping me see the similarities between his life and mine. I was very impressed by how David, the King was such a loving man toward God, family, friends, and the people under his reign. But then I would struggle again in believing that God could use me this way, writing my life story and sharing it. I did not understand how I could write the story of my life if I were in my third marriage and struggling with this one too. What could I write? That I have many problems in this marriage and that I have failed in another love relationship again?

I knew God could still use me, but I wanted to keep being used in the way I was used to, which was at a small scale and without exposing my personal life and the intimate details about it. I always tried to share my life testimonies so I could encourage others, but I did not realize that I was hiding the things I was ashamed of, and this was keeping me filled with fear. By writing a book and publishing it meant that people would know my life story, and that was what I struggled with.

There was a day that the house needed some work, so my husband hired a man that we knew from church to help him with the work. During a break, I had the opportunity to talk with this man for a while. I have known him for many years since my kids were little. While talking with him, he shared with me that he was helping a friend on how to write a book. Then I shared about how God was giving me writings and but was struggling to write my life story since I did not think I was a good testimony to follow.

He then encouraged me to share my story. He knew I was passionate about God but said that sharing my failures could help other people. He mentioned that he knew of someone who was at a crucial time in his life and in need of making the right decision and could use my testimony. After he said that, I felt very encouraged about sharing my life story.

God was faithful. He never let me go but continued working in me and showing me why I had to obey him, and after a few weeks, I obeyed and accepted his will for my life. I will write my life story and publish it. This was not easy because my marriage problems kept getting worse. I faced many hard days and struggled but would feel prompted by God to insist on meditating on the life of David, the King from the Bible. So, I read again the Bible and took a closer look at David's life and his sins and failures, not just the good things. I was forced to see his full humanity and not just the great things he did. Then I was able to see what God saw in David despite his faults and sins!

Oh, yes, King David was a man of God, but he also was human with failures and temptations and who sometimes failed into sin. This same David had been a great warrior, a shepherd, poet, writer, musician, teacher, leader with a strong will and mind, and much more.

When David was confronted with his sin, he would repent and accept God's discipline. I was reminded that this king was that child who one day believed he could kill a giant with a rock despite his family and people not believing in him. He did it! He killed the giant! And God had chosen him to be king, so everything he would live in his life before his reign was used for when he became king! He became King David, and he kept the kingdom and leadership until his death!

King David never lost his kingdom. He fulfilled his calling and purpose in life! The bible speaks of him and his lineage in Matthew 1:1, "The book of the generation of Jesus Christ, the son of David, the son of Abraham." David was a king, ruler over God's people from where the Messiah, Jesus Christ, would come! Joseph, a descendant of David, was the father of Jesus. David's life brought glory to God! That is JESUS CHRIST'S lineage!

I Have Something to Offer!

Around the end of August, I had the opportunity to help another young person, this time a young lady who needed guidance regarding her dreams and spiritual life. With my husband's approval, I invited this young woman, with her mother, to spend three days at my home. I spent time helping this family while my husband was working so it would not affect our family time. Through the years, I helped people stay at my home because they needed a temporary place to live and transportation or because they were sick or alone. And in my years of ministry, I have been able to give counseling for an hour or a little more, but typically I have done this at their or my home or the church in Tijuana. I was now hosting, for the first time, a family so I could be their counselor and mentor. When I worked with this young lady, I shared a little of my testimony, which made me realize that my life testimony could have a positive impact on someone's life. I received more affirmation after I shared with them one of my writings because they gave me such positive feedback.

The experience with this family made me visualize my life as a speaker and mentor, that I could be professionally helping people. This thought brought great satisfaction to my soul. Now I needed to figure out how to make these dreams come true, which isn't easy. Perhaps it was more feasible to get a normal job and ignore all these plans, but I didn't want to do it because I knew that for this purpose I was born and I longed so much to fulfill it and see it come true. It only required a lot of faith on my part to see the impossible made possible. When I longed to become a speaker and a mentor while attending college, I thought about working on a nonprofit program, but now everything had changed. I would need to be doing this type of work as self-employed, which can be much harder. There is so much going on in my personal life that I could not focus on writing but focus on our move.

The move was not difficult for me, but it was difficult for my husband. I was patient and gave him my understanding and support because I know how difficult it is having to move and especially because of the emotional impact that this move had on him. We moved into an apartment, and once we settled in, I focused on making it our new home. I cooked and tended to my family as usual. As for my husband, he acted so negatively toward this new home and constantly made me see that this place was not his house, let alone his home. This hurt me a lot. He could not see how much I loved him and that my son and I were looking forward for him to feel at home, just like us.

I hadn't had any success with him. No matter what I said or not, he still disliked having to live in a new place. This kept him in a constantly bad mood. I could see that his brokenness was caused by grieving and the changes in his life too. I believed that I could help him change and heal since I had struggled with some of the same issues in my past, but I was so wrong. He was not even open to accept any help or recognize his struggles.

Since we moved into this apartment, all our problems escalated, and our disagreements were no longer so sporadic but often and always becoming fights and ending always with my husband's abandonment. We were living like this for around five months until my husband left for good. So now I found myself in this whole mess and alone. Where is that love that I so much desired to have from a man? That man is my husband, and I should have his love. Where is my husband if you ask me? I will answer you; he is not with me!

PART TWO

WHO CHOSE YOU?

California, February 2, 2017

Continuation of day 1 out of 7. But today I was alone in this apartment and with my only hope in God and in this fasting that I started today. I knew I could no longer live the way we used to, and I knew that despite how hard our separation was, we needed it. My disobedience to God caused sufferings and failures in two marriages, and now I found myself fighting for my third marriage. I could see which type of woman I had been. Now I saw the battle between my flesh and spirit, one side feeding the flesh, the sexual desires and more.

On the other side, the spiritual was feeding the spirit and just wanting to be at Jesus's feet and doing his will. I wanted to be happy with my husband, and I knew he desired the same, even though at this time we did not know how to make it possible. We did not enter this marriage with malice, but we entered because we fell in love and were seeking love and company, but so far, we had not had much of this over the past few months.

The fact was that we were two broken people carrying much pain, which was affecting us to be able to show, give, and receive love. I could surely rest knowing that God was merciful, and even though I was going through these difficulties, He would use this marriage for our good and his glory.

I see which actions and decisions I have taken in my life, and it is incredible all the suffering that I have caused to myself and others. I see also the people who have caused me many sufferings because I allowed them in my life and those who came in by force. I never realized how fragile I had been in my life until today. During my whole life, I thought I was a strong woman, but now I see how easy it was for me to give in to a man in my life and sin. I did not know what a heavy burden I was carrying and that I was not forgetting or forgiving.

Every time I fought with my husband, I would bring into the present my feelings of resentment toward men, which were based on my pains and lack of forgiveness. These feelings were so negative toward men, so therefore they were negative toward my husband. Other things came out because of doing this list too. I not only confronted my past, but I accepted it as part of who I am and who it made me be. No one else lived this life but me, and only I had overcome it!

I ended this long list of my past and finished it today, the first day of my seven-day fast at the age of my middle forties. It took so many years to do this but thank God it is now over! By looking into my life and all my sufferings, it gives me compassion for myself, which moves me to love myself and give myself much grace. I am in so much need of all that because I had lived a life as a broken person for so long. But no more. Thank God! I see how much of a godly woman I am but how I just struggled on being in the spirit since I didn't know how to do it.

I am so glad I had to face my past because I could not see these positive things about me before. Also, by doing this list, I now have more compassion for my children, to love them to the fullest because they need all the love I could give them and extend them much grace too and understanding. Now for my husband, I have compassion too. I can see how I have been trying to love him but doing it the wrong way, so now I must love him the right way as my soul mate. I must extend him grace and understanding too and learn how to be that helpmate. And lastly it gives me compassion for those who I have hurt.

Who Chose You?

What man is he that feareth the Lord? him shall He teach in the
way that he shall choose. His soul shall dwell at ease; and his seed
shall inherit the earth. The secret of the Lord is with them that
fear Him; and He will shew them his covenant. Mine eyes are
ever toward the Lord; for He shall pluck my feet out of the net.
—Psalm 25:12–15

I spent time praying, asking the Lord for forgiveness and deliverance where I need it. I know that God had heard my prayer. I accepted his forgiveness and deliverance. Then I prayed, surrendering all my sufferings and pains to God and asking Him to heal me. As for my husband, I know he is fragile too. He has suffered in his life and needs to heal too. We may not have the same sufferings, but he is human just like me, so we are both susceptible to the pains of life and struggles of the flesh. We have both sinned and received and caused pain in our lives as imperfect beings that we are. But we have a perfect God, and this gives me hope!

The devil has always wanted to destroy me. It was not enough for Satan to steal my innocence and childhood, pervert my sexuality and my mind, and rob me of many blessings, but he wanted to kill me, but he cannot because I belong to Jesus Christ! Now God reminds me that he created me, so therefore he knows what is best for me, for he is God. He tells me in Job 38:1–4,

> Then the Lord answered Job (Delilah) out of the whirlwind, and said, Who is this that darkeneth counsel by words without knowledge? Gird up now thy loins like a man (woman); for I will demand of thee and answer thou me. Where wast thou when I laid the foundations of the earth? declare, if thou hast understanding.

Then He tells me in Psalm 100:3–5,

> Know ye that the Lord he is God: it is He that hath made us, and not we ourselves; we are his people, and the sheep of his pasture. Enter into his gates with thanksgiving, and into his courts with praise: be thankful unto Him and bless his name. For the Lord is good; his mercy is everlasting; and his truth endureth to all generations.

The Lord reminds me of what He did for me on the cross with this verse in Matthew 27:27–31,

> Then the soldiers of the governor took Jesus into the common hall and gathered unto Him the whole band of soldiers. And they stripped Him and put on Him a scarlet robe. And when they had platted a crown of thorns, they put it upon his head, and a reed in his right hand: and they bowed the knee before Him, and mocked Him, saying, Hail, King of the Jews! And they spit upon Him, and took the reed, and smote Him on the head. And after that they had mocked Him, they took the robe off from Him, and put his own raiment on Him, and led Him away to crucify Him.

Delilah P.I.O.

In addition, God shows me how I did not understand what marriage is, what it means, and why he established it. He makes me see that despite praying and yearning to have a good marriage for so many years, I have been very ignorant about the real meaning of marriage. I have not lacked examples of committed Christian marriages, but mine has been failure after failure. Although I want so much to be happy and bring honor to God in my third marriage, I lost sight, vision, and focus of God in my marriage. So, God tells me in Psalm 127:1, "Except the Lord build the house, they labour in vain that build it."

How sad is for me to realize that it was useless to have a place to live, cook, and keep clean if the marriage isn't being fully built on God's foundation. I am married but abandoned! I am here in my house sleeping in my living room on a couch instead of my bedroom. My bedroom is empty with just a few boxes with my personal stuff and my clothes in the closet. My room is empty, as there was neither a bed nor a husband.

Despite this depressive scene, God wants me to think about how I had been praying for revival and marriages for few years since when I was living in the American state of Missouri. Although at that time I was separated and going through the end of my second marriage, I felt led by God to pray for revival and marriages. And these were the verses that God showed me at that time:

- "Wherefore he saith, Awake thou that sleepest, and arise from the dead, and CHRIST shall give thee light" (Ephesians 5:14).
- "My people (The Body of Christ-The Bride-The Church) are destroyed for lack of knowledge (the Word of God) because thou hast rejected knowledge" (Hosea 4:6).

I had been praying for a few years for marriages and revival but without understanding fully what they mean to God until today, when he revealed it to me. The Christian people are drinking milk when they must be eating meat. This needs to be transformed for revival to come! Yes, the Christians need to change and eat meat (spiritual maturity) and not milk (no spiritual growth). This lack of knowledge prevents the bride (the Christian, the church) from getting ready and being ready daily. How will the bride (the believer, the church) be ready if she lacks much of her biblical foundation or if she does not live based on God's Word? This bride (the believer, the church) needs to act. So, she needs to get up and not sit like a baby, waiting for her bottle of milk but be eating meat, the Word of God, the Word and only the Word of God, the verb that was made flesh, Jesus Christ!

I am included in this exhortation because sometimes I drank milk and other times, I ate meat. I struggle on staying strong when going through trials in my life or when tempted. So, after this revelation, I answered God, "And Mary (Delilah) said, Behold the handmaid of the Lord; be it unto me according to thy Word" (Luke 1:38).

Then God showed me this. Although I chose my own destiny, He still loves me and created me with a purpose. He made me see that I am someone special on earth and that I belong to a family. His purpose for my life has always been there since God remains, and his blessings are still in force despite my sufferings, sins, and bad decisions in my life. Led by the Lord, I wrote my name and filled it with all my information.

Graphic 2: My Name, Who Am I?

Jeremiah 1:5	D	E	L	I	L	A H
Before I formed thee in the belly I knew thee; and before thou camest forth out of the womb I sanctified thee, and I ordained thee a prophet unto the nations.	Date of birth: Daughter of: Sister:	Date of salvation: Date of my calling:	Wife of: Mother of:	Daughter-in-law:	Niece of: Aunt: Sister-in-law of:	Friend of: Neighbor:

I am somebody! I belong to a great family and community, and I am not alone! God led me to read these Bible verses: Matthew 26:26–30; Isaiah

54; and Revelation 12:11, 16:15, 19:9, 22:16–17. Then I took communion at home this evening and thank God for all his revelations for my life. I am asking him to help me believe in his Word so I could walk in it. I am not strong and need his help. Later in the evening, I attended a prayer meeting at church, where I prayed for others and received prayer for my family. This gave me much strength.

In Whose Hands?

Before my day was over, I was able to give my marriage to God, believing that God established marriage and that He will do what He needs to do in my husband and me. But before I could totally release my marriage to God, He had to speak to me and give me his peace, and this is how it happened.

I took a walk in the afternoon, and I used that time to talk to God in prayer. I was crying while praying when I heard God telling, "Trust in Me."

With a crying voice, I answered, "Lord, I can't stop crying because I don't have my husband with me. I lost him."

Then God said to me," Stop crying and trust Me."

But I kept crying and went back and forth with God with the same answer, and He would tell me the same answer too, to leave my husband in his hands.

Until I was finally able to release my husband in God's hand, I said, "God, I lost both of my children when they were little, and you gave them back to me. So, I now release my husband in your hands. And I know that you cannot give him back to me until he is the man, he needs to be for you and then for me." After doing this I was inconsolable because I felt I was losing my husband.

So, God asked me, "Delilah, what do I do with everything you put in my hands? Don't I bless everything that you leave in my hands? I always bless everything you leave in my hands."

This answer of God made me realize that it is so true: he had always blessed everything I leave in his hands. I was able to get my children back and raise them. God has always blessed me and my family and always provided for us. After this conversation, I went home, and the Lord led me to read "Therefore I say unto you, What things soever ye desire, when ye pray, believe that ye receive them, and ye shall have them" (Mark 11:24) and "Ask, and it shall be given you; seek, and ye shall find; knock, and it shall be opened unto you" (Matthew 7:7).

After reading this last verse, I was able to leave my husband and marriage in God's hands. Now I could focus on what God wants me to do, so I spoke Exodus 3:13–15,

> And Moses (Delilah) said unto God, Behold, when I come unto the children of Israel, and shall say unto them, The God of your fathers hath sent me unto you; and they shall say to me, what is his name? what shall I say unto them? And God said unto Moses (Delilah), I AM THAT I AM: and He said, thus shalt thou say unto the children of Israel, I AM hath sent me unto you. And God said moreover unto Moses (Delilah), Thus shalt thou say unto the children of Israel, the Lord God of your fathers, the God of Abraham, the God of Isaac, and the God of Jacob, hath sent me unto you: this is my name for ever, and this is my memorial unto all generations.

Joshua 1:5 reads, "So, I will be with thee: I will not fail thee, nor forsake thee (Delilah) and Matthew 28:19 Go ye therefore, and teach all nations, baptizing them in the name of the Father, and of the Son, and of the Holy Ghost."

So, God gave me encouragement through his Word, and I was able to rise from the dead and believe in revival for my life and marriage, despite my present circumstances. I had to seek the knowledge of God and not mine! I needed to be more in the Word, the Bible, so I could make God my guide and put all my faith in Jesus Christ! Everything revealed in my past was not for condemnation, but for God to show me how I have sinned and not to do it again and to rid me of being ashamed and deliver me from the oppression of the enemy.

I needed to learn to not just forgive those who hurt me, but I needed to let go, to forget it all. These sufferings were causing the heaviness in my spirit and keeping me from not seeing and accepting my present life. Now the Lord exhorts me with these Bible verses: Galatians 5:1–26, Ephesians 5:5–7 and Hebrews 10:38–39.

> Ephesians 5:5–7 reads, "For this ye know, that no whoremonger, nor unclean person, nor covetous man, who is an idolater, hath any inheritance in the kingdom of Christ and of God. Let no man deceive you with vain words: for because of these things cometh the wrath of God upon the children of disobedience. Be not ye therefore partakers with them."

Galatians 5:24–25 reads, "And they that are Christ's have crucified the flesh with the affections and lusts. If we live in the Spirit, let us also walk in the Spirit."

Today You Exist!

God gives me encouragement by showing me the life of Abraham and his faith. What a blessing! I see the faults of Abraham and Sarah, but above all, I can see that God fulfilled his promises given to Abraham and Sarah, although the wait time was long. This is a testimony that God is using to lift me and move forward in my walk with Christ, despite my present circumstances in my life. God was real in the life of Abraham and Sarah. Let us look at these verses:

- Jehovah Speaks: Genesis 12:1–3, 15:1–5
- Jehovah Visits: Genesis 21:1
- Jehovah Interrogates: Genesis 18:9,13
- Jehovah Promises: Genesis 12:2–3, 13:15–17, 18:10
- Jehovah Appears: Genesis 18:1
- Jehovah Fulfills: Genesis 21:1-2

"And he believed the Lord; and he counted it to him for righteousness" (Genesis 15:6).

God gave Abraham the promise of the Promised Land at the age of seventy-five. Before he turned eighty-six, he was promised that he would be a father and have innumerable descendants. Abraham became a father for the first time at the age of eighty-six, and by this time, he had already been living in the Promised Land of Canaan for ten years. However, the son of the promise would not arrive until Abraham was ninety-nine years old. So, he had to wait twenty-five years for his promised son, Isaac. Let us look into their lives.

God changed Abram's name to Abraham, the father of nations and from whom kings will come from. It was to Abraham that God gave the promise for Israel, God's chosen people. He was a man strong in his faith to the Lord, but there would be times where he would be weak because he let his flesh lead him to sin. Abraham loved the Lord, but at times he had disbelief and would let his wife, Sarah, make decisions that he should have made.

Sarah would lead Abraham to adultery and to father a child that was not the promised child, all due to her impatience and Abraham's obedience to her instead of obeying God. Abraham would hear God speak to him and would have conversations with him and his angels, but neither to say he still disbelieved and sinned. He would lie about Sarah being his wife when he was in Egypt because he thought they would kill him. So, he acted out of fear. Would you call that faith? Why is he counted in the Bible in the book of James as the father of faith? We see that Abraham had so many faults, and we probably could have a list of all his wrongdoings.

But I want to get your attention by looking into why Abram was chosen. He was a sinner just like you and me, but when God spoke to Abraham and told him to do something for him, he would do it. Abraham obeyed. The times he got in trouble was not because God did not tell him what he was going to do for him and with him, but it was while he was waiting on God. Abraham was being motivated by certain things and people in his life like his age, spouse, desires, doubt, and disobedience, which is what made him fall into sin.

The great example of Abraham is not that he did not fall, but every time he failed, he would get up. He would repent from his sin and walk back with God. The promise given to Abraham would not come without suffering though. This man endured many trials and tribulations as he was on his way to the Promised Land, but God was with him and every generation of Abraham. God never changed even though the generations were different. He gave the promise to Abraham and kept his Word and fulfilled it. God never told him that his promise would arrive without problems and that it would be easy.

On the contrary, God told him ahead of time that the generations would arrive at the Promised Land, but it would cost them their freedom, and He even told him which generations would suffer it. It was up to Abraham to believe the promise and keep on following God despite knowing that he would not see it all, but only his future generations would see. He obeyed because he loved God and his parents. He obeyed out of the love of God and the love for his future generations. Despite that, he would never see all the promises fulfilled in his lifetime. He believed in God, and by doing so, he blessed all his generations for life! This is the reason why he is called "the Father of Faith."

When I study the life of Abraham and Sarah, I see why the promised son took a long time to come. I see why they suffered so much, starting with Sarah, Abraham, and those around him. But I also see how the mercy of God held and protected them and supplied their needs despite their failures. God's plans and purpose for their lives were fulfilled.

Let us see how Sarah's submission benefits her, Abraham, and their descendants. Genesis 18:9 reads, "And they said unto him, Where is Sarah thy wife? And he said, Behold, in the tent." Under the roof and covering of Abraham, Sarah was able to receive a blessing because she was in the perfect place, her home. The descendants of their marriage exist until today! God fulfilled and continues to fulfill his promises made to their marriage! So as promises were fulfilled to them, so will God's promises be fulfilled in my life! I need to remain in my house, which is my home, even if my husband is not with me. I exist until today, and the promises of God have been fulfilled and will continue to be fulfilled in my life, marriage, and descendants! Psalm 100 reads,

> Make a joyful noise unto the Lord, all ye lands. Serve the Lord with gladness: come before his presence with singing. Know ye that the Lord He is God: it is He that hath made us, and not we ourselves; we are his people, and the sheep of his pasture. Enter into his gates with thanksgiving, and into his courts with praise be thankful unto Him and bless his name. For the Lord is good; his mercy is everlasting; and his truth endureth to all Generations.

Chapter 2

THREATS OF THE ENEMY AND GOD'S PROTECTION

But the men put forth their hand, and pulled Lot into the house to them, and shut to the door. And they smote the men that were at the door of the house with blindness, both small and great: so that they wearied themselves to find the door.
—Genesis 19:10–11

Day 2 out of 7. Is Friday, is my second day of prayer and fasting. I started my day as normal, dropping off my son at school and then returning home. I continued to study the Bible and prayed that God would show me his will and that I would focus on him and not the circumstances of my marriage. God gives me peace and shows me that I needed to keep the communication open with my husband if there were to be respect.

I received a text from my husband that contained a picture of his lunch. He had no idea that I was fasting. What a temptation, but thank God that he kept me strong to continue with my fast. My obedience to God is more important than a meal. God was going to use this fasting for him to liberate me and do his will in my life, so I needed to keep going.

On these seven days, I had given up on eating solid food, going to the movies, and watching TV. I intended to stay home as much I could. I was only going to drink liquids like juice, tea, decaf coffee, and water and eat snacks like fruits and small portions of bread or crackers. Only with this fast could I get rid of what distracted me from listening to God, and then I could spend more time reading his Word and listening to his voice. Believe me, it is not easy to give up all food, especially what you want, and accept what God wants you to do and eat during this time.

Having to give up watching TV, talking to friends and shopping, or going to the movies is not easy, but I was going to do it with God's help. I knew that I must do this fast since God asked me to, giving up food I liked and my routine but instead focusing only on God while my son was away at school. I already suffered a lot and did things my way, so I did not want to live like this anymore. I needed to depend on God completely, and that was the only way I can have victory in Jesus.

I like to cook and eat homemade meals so much that I desire to one day open a restaurant. So, this fast was not an easy thing but was possible with God, who keeps me from falling into temptation but helps me stay focused on Him.

The Door

But the men put forth their hand, and pulled Lot into the house
to them, and shut to the door. And they smote the men that
were at the door of the house with blindness, both small and
great: so that they wearied themselves to find the door.
—Genesis 19:10–11

God showed me two examples of how to protect us as He closes
the door against Satan and his demons. For God to protect us, it was
important to be obedient. Also, I saw how God shows mercy when we
are disobedient. Proof of this is my life, but now let us look at the lives of
Abraham and Lot, who lived together and then in separate regions.

Abraham: 1 Samuel 2:6; Genesis 9:5–6, 20:1–18; Exodus 20:13; Matthew 5:21

Abraham offered his only son, Isaac, in sacrifice as an act of obedience
to God. God then closed the door of death to Isaac on that day. He would

die a natural death later in life and not by his father's hand. God told Abraham to take Isaac and offer him as a sacrifice, but he did not say to kill him. Because of the obedience of Abraham, God opened the door for an animal to take Isaac's place of sacrifice. God would not allow Isaac to be killed by his father and by doing so commit the sin of murder.

The obedience of Abraham led him to take his promised son to the mountain on that day, and because of his obedience, he was blessed by being before the presence of God. This was the day when Abraham got to know God as Jehovah-Jireh (The Provider) for the first time. And on this day, God told Abraham that he and his offspring would possess the gates of their enemies.

On another occasion, God closed the door of adultery to avoid another man, King Abimelech, sleeping with Sarah, the wife of Abraham. Even though Abraham had lied, saying that she was his sister and not his wife, God would speak to the king in a dream, telling him to let go of Sarah and the instructions that would follow upon her release.

God did not allow sin against himself and for Sarah to be offended. So instead of being mocked, God is honored, and so is Sarah. God opened the doors of blessing for her and Abraham as they departed that city safe and full of riches. And even the deceived king came out blessed as God opened the door of life, and now children were procreated in the king's house.

Lot: Genesis 14:1–16, 18:16–22, 19:1–16

When Lot and his family were kidnapped, God closed the door of wickedness against Lot, his family, and possessions. God sent Abraham and 318 servants to rescue Lot from his enemy's hands. Then a second threat came to Lot and his family, this time by the people in his city of Sodom. The perverted people of Sodom went to Lot's home in search of his two visitors, the two angels. To try to save the angels from perversion, Lot offered his own daughters, but this would be sinful, and it was never an option. The angels did not need Lot's help because they are celestial beings who depend directly on God. For we see that the angels rejected Lot's help and did what God sent them to do, to close the door of wickedness that came against Lot and his family. God closed the door of sin against Lot and his daughters. God also stopped Lot from committing sin, yes, because

Lot had offered his daughters to perversion. God punished the wicked by having the angel blind them and then closed the door on their faces.

We may think that we can help God, but as we see in this story, God did not need Lot's help. And God does not need any human being's help also! And just like Lot, if we try to help God, we will do things wrong, just as Lot was trying to do, wrong and sinful. We must trust God because He is the only one who knows it all, so He is the only one who can protect us from the enemy.

Chapter 3

MY WEAKNESS AND TEMPTATIONS

Even so the tongue is a little member, and boasteth great things. Behold, how great a matter a little fire kindleth! And the tongue is a fire, a world of iniquity: so is the tongue among our members, that it defileth the whole body, and setteth on fire the course of nature; and it is set on fire of hell.
—James 3:5–6

Day 3 out of 7. Is Saturday, and my son and I stayed home since he had no sports practices. We ate breakfast together. He ate his normal breakfast, and I had my fasting portion. I spent time reading the Bible and praying. Earlier this morning, my husband had sent me a text message in which he expressed how he felt. We have hurt each other so much. I could see how much I had hurt him and pushed him out of my life. I saw that I had hurt God first and then my husband, how I always blamed him for my faults and sins. I had told him that because of him, I could not put myself to write and watch my diet. All these were Satan's lies that I, Delilah, the daughter of God, had believed. I thought, *No wonder why I find myself where I am today. That is why I am all alone, without my bed and my husband. No wonder I've been depressed, without hope and purpose.*

I read the verses in Matthew 26:33–35, 57–75. God shows me through the life of Peter how I struggled just like Peter in being in the flesh, having a carnal tongue. Peter denied Jesus three times before the rooster crowed. Though he loved Jesus and said with his own words that he would not deny him, Peter failed.

As a human being, I had many struggles that when tempted, I would fall into sin, sinning against God and my husband and sons. As a mother, I had failed and hurt them with my control, being judgmental, impatient, and capricious. I lacked submission to God and husband, a lack of God's wisdom and trust. I thought I was strong and would not fall, but I did. I failed. I was depending on my pride, and I could not see that I was weak, and just like Peter, I failed. Thank God it was not guilt, remorse and pity that I felt because that is what the enemy of our soul wants us to feel. No, I felt the Holy Spirit's conviction, so I repented and asked God to forgive me and walk away from those sins. I knew that I might be strong spiritually in many areas of my life, but today was about seeing in which areas I was weak and which temptations I struggled with.

My tongue has been a problem since childhood because I talked a lot and used my tongue to be defensive, and I continue to be that way into my adulthood without realizing it. I was raised in a large family, and most of us talked a lot, so I did not think that being talkative would be wrong. About five years ago, I realized that I talked very much and that many times it was just because I was expressing my thoughts. I needed to learn to keep my thoughts to myself and know when to share them and not to just open my mouth. And that was the time when I started praying that God would give me control over my tongue and have a better choice of words.

As a child, I did not hurt much with it, but as I grew, I did, especially as an adult. Peter with his tongue denied Jesus, and I, Delilah, have done the same by using my mouth for evil. So, from now on, I will be more sensitive to God to see the dangerous power of my tongue. The Lord gives me this verse in James 3:5–6,

> Even so the tongue is a little member, and boasteth great things. Behold, how great a matter a little fire kindleth! And the tongue is a fire, a world of iniquity: so is the tongue among our members, that it defileth the whole body, and setteth on fire the course of nature; and it is set on fire of hell.

Broken by what God showed me, I asked for his forgiveness, and I knew I had to ask my husband and children for forgiveness too. So, I sent a text to my husband, asking if we could meet on his lunch break to talk. At 12:30 p.m., I checked the outside mail, and then I saw my husband approaching in his car. He got out of the car, looked me in the eye, and gave me a big hug. He said he had not read my text because he was driving, but he just wanted to see me. We agreed to meet that day at lunchtime. By now we had been separated for seven days, the longest time of separation that we ever had.

We met at lunchtime, and I shared with him what God had shown me in the Bible about Peter's life and mine. I shared with him the graphic 1 in chapter 1 and asked him to forgive me for being a woman in the flesh many times, to forgive me for not submitting to him and failing him. I let him know that I loved him, and I wanted to stay married to him. I had to accept responsibility for my faults as a wife, without excuses, and I did it with a sincere heart.

My husband forgave me but expressed his doubts about if we should stay together since we were so different. He thought this way and not just him because I used to think that too, that we were a mistake, but no longer because God showed me what marriage means to him and what mine needs to be.

As hard as it was, I had to sit and listen to my husband explain his negative feeling toward the marriage and me. I had to give him the opportunity to express himself. He continued to talk, bringing up all the bad things I had done and my failures, so I subtly asked him to stop reminding me of my failures and to focus on the now. I shared with him how God had told me to fast for seven days. During the process I find myself in now, God showed me what marriage means to Him.

At the end of our conversation, I felt peace and said that I respected how he felt. I said, "Come home when you're ready, and I'll wait on God."

I asked him if I could pray, and with his permission, I anointed his head with oil and prayed for God's will in his life. I prayed for God to give him peace and to fulfill God's purpose for his life. I also gave thanks to God for allowing me to pray for my husband even though he doubted my repented heart and our marriage. I gave thanks to my husband for listening and allowing me to pray for him. We said goodbye, and I went home.

When I got home, I shared with Moses the Bible study of Peter's life and the similarities with my life. He listened very patiently, and once I was done, I asked him to forgive me, and he did. Without reproach, he hugged me, and I began to cry with gratitude for having a son with such a noble heart. I prayed and anointed him with oil, asking God to fulfill his purpose in his life and to bless him.

When the night came, I called Gershom and shared with him the same thing I had shared with my husband and younger son. I told him how God had given me conviction. We had a long conversation, and of course my son forgave me. He was happy for me for what God had shown me and that I was willing to accept my faults and how I was willing to change. Before I finished this call, my son shared with me that he was very worried and stressed about the pending payments for his school tuition at his university. He was a full-time student and worked part time, and as parents, we helped him as much as we could.

God showed me that this was Satan's oppression, that he was the one who was tempting my son to disobey God in losing his faith and filling it with doubt. I asked my son to wait on God to provide and said that there was no need to entertain the thought about quitting school. Doing that would be acting prematurely, and it is best to wait and trust God. Finally, my son came to reason, and I felt calm and was able to pray with him. I told him that God would provide for him, as He has always done, and that He never fails us.

Thank God my son shared what was in his heart. The Lord answered my mother's prayer. I reached out to his dad that same night and asked him to call Gershom. The next day I had a voice mail from my son saying, "Mom, I'm fine, and I love you very much."

Thank God that as parents we can pray for our children, no matter how old they are, and they can know that we are here to guide them. They still need our guidance, even if they no longer live at home. It does not matter what decision they make. My sons know that I will pray first and then try to help them. Intercessory prayer is powerful! GOD is good!

The next person on my list to ask for forgiveness was my sister-in-law and her husband, my brother the pastor. I asked them to forgive me for sometimes intruding in their lives. No matter how good I thought my intentions were, I needed to give them space and not intrude in their way of living. I was sorry for taking away my brother from his family time when it was not necessary, as many times we just talked, and that could be done any other day. It was not wrong for us to meet to talk and spend time as families do, but the trouble was that both of us are very talkative people, and so on many occasions we would talk too much on the phone or in person. We come from a big family, and he is my only sibling who lives close to me since the rest of my family is far away.

No matter how lonely I feel, oftentimes I must learn to give space to my brother and his family. Both forgave me and prayed for me. They expressed how happy they were that God had spoken to me and reminded me how he always forgives us.

They encouraged me to always go to God with my weaknesses and temptations, as he is the one who can help me change and move forward. They reminded me that my tongue could often start out as a good conversation, but at the end of my talking, I could be complaining and be negative, so to watch my tongue. Often, we hurt those who we love and are close to us, and then this causes us to push them out of our lives. This has been so true in my life, and I had not realized it until God showed me.

I have a great relationship with my brother, and I will keep having it, but now I would be more respectful of their family space and my place as his sister. I do miss the large family I grew with and wish we were all close to each other, but that is not possible. So, I must learn to give God my need of wanting to be close to my family and have him fill me up with his love. In the meantime, I will keep cultivating a good family bond with all my family as much as it's possible. Realizing how much I miss my family caused me to pray for them.

Before the night was over, I did a graphic, a genogram of my family starting with my grandparents and ending it with my sons. (An example of this graphic is on my webpage.) Then I used it to intercede for my family by praying and declaring God's blessings upon my family. Then I prayed for my friends, the church, and Israel. I finished my fast and prayer this day by submitting to God, my Creator, my whole body, soul, and spirit.

Chapter 4

I FORGIVE MYSELF

It is better to dwell in a corner of the housetop, than
with a brawling woman in a wide house.
—Proverbs 21:9

Day 4 out of 7. Is Sunday, and God kept me on the same path of healing, asking for forgiveness to those I hurt. I called my mother, who lives in Mexico, and asked her to forgive me.

She replied, "I forgive you, daughter, and I love you very much."

I then sent a text to my siblings who all lived outside of the United States and asked for their forgiveness and then went to the church service. Before the service started, I was able to read the reply that one of my brothers sent.

He said, "Nobody is perfect, and I don't condemn you."

I thought that my brother had misunderstood my text because he thought I felt guilt, but I thought I had sent a different message, of repentance.

Then another brother had recorded a video in which he told me, "There is nothing to forgive, and only God does that. He is the only judge. You are the one who needs to forgive yourself."

I started to cry, realizing that the text I had sent them reflected guilt and that I had not forgiven myself.

This same brother told me, "Delilah, God is the one who has to forgive you. You are the one who has to forgive yourself. Your husband and your sons are the ones who have to forgive you, but not us. We love you just the way you are with your crazy personality!"

I cried and said aloud, "I FORGIVE MYSELF!"

And I felt free! I felt as if I had dumped a hundred pounds off my back. Minutes later, the service started, and I was praising God with each song. I was opened to receive the message of God taught by our pastor, and this message went along with what I was experiencing in my life. Once the service was done, I realized that I was broken into pieces and that I had been humbled by God. This was one more process I needed to experience, and it was for my good.

I then prayed and said, "I'M READY! USE ME!"

I went home, and after I parked my car, God answered my prayer, He said, "Delilah, you have been disobedient. You let other things and people take My place in your life."

I said to him, "Lord, I lost my children, and you returned them. I lost my husband, but I leave him in your hands, no matter what. Here is your prodigal daughter again with two sons and without my husband. You have never left me. Use me, Jesus!"

Then God gave me these two verses:

If my people, which are called by my name, shall humble themselves, and pray, and seek my face, and turn from their wicked ways; then will I hear from heaven, and will forgive their sin, and will heal their land. Now mine eyes shall be open, and mine ears attent unto the prayer that is made in this place. For now have I chosen and sanctified this house, that my name may be there forever: and mine eyes and mine heart shall be there perpetually. And as for thee, if thou wilt walk before me, as David thy father walked, and do according to all that I have commanded thee, and shalt observe my statutes and my judgments; Then will I stablish the throne of thy kingdom, according as I have covenanted with David thy father, saying, There shall not fail thee a man to be ruler in Israel. (2 Chronicles 7:14–18)

He will not suffer thy foot to be moved: He that keepeth thee will not slumber. Behold, He that keepeth Israel shall neither slumber nor sleep. The Lord is thy keeper: the Lord is thy shade upon thy right hand. The sun shall not smite thee by day, nor the moon by night. The Lord shall preserve thee from all evil: He shall preserve thy soul. The Lord shall preserve thy going out and thy coming in from this time forth, and even for evermore. (Psalm 121:3–8)

After these revelations of God, I was at peace and enjoyed the rest of my day with my son and some company, a family visit. I made them supper, but I continued with my fast. I watched some TV with them even though I had given up watching TV during this fast. God gave me peace of sitting down and watching cartoons with the kids.

God said to me, "This is my love, and this is how you show my love. I do not want your religion and sacrifices, but your love for Me and Others. You will have peace this way! Enjoy your day with your family. Be yourself and not a religious woman! Dance and be merry!"

I understood that it was not about what I was giving up on doing this week, but it was about having my heart right. Yes, about having peace with myself, God, and those around me. What a blessed day!

Chapter 5

SPEAKING LIFE

Pleasant words are as an honeycomb, sweet to
the soul, and health to the bones.
—Proverbs 16:24

Day 5 out of 7. Is Monday, and I spoke with Gershom about his concerns regarding his college tuition. After we spoke, I was able to give those concerns to God. I asked for him to take control and to show me how to pray for my son. I prayed for God's favor and provision for my son's life, for him to have peace and to wait on him. Praying made me realize that I needed to intercede more in prayers for my sons. This afternoon, as usual, I picked up my son at 5:00 p.m. from high school, but this time we went to the store instead of going home.

Moses needed something from the store, and while I was there, Gershom's father called. He shared with me that they were lies of the enemy of our souls who had attacked our son the other day. I totally agreed with him. I then shared with him how I had always struggled because I lived believing those lies of the enemy, but no more. I told him that God had reminded me not to believe the enemy but to believe the truth, God's Word, and to obey him.

I then shared with my son's father how I felt so bad for messing up the lives of my children. I told him I had messed up badly, and they had suffered on my account and had problematic lives.

He replied, "Delilah, you have not caused problematic lives. You are a great mother. You are a great woman with great sons and a great family! Life is in the tongue. Don't think negatively but speak life!"

These words made me realize that this was a continuation of my process of healing and deliverance. One day before, God had shown me my carnal tongue, and today was the continuation of what I needed to be fully released from guilt. For most of my children's lives, I had lived believing that I had failed them. Therefore, I thought I had destroyed their lives. Now I could see that that was not the case at all! I thanked him for exhorting me, encouraging me, and keeping us in his prayers. It is not easy to change your mind, and I was tested very soon.

When I was driving my son back home from the store, I felt irritable and immediately began to think negatively, and by the time I arrived home and parked the car, I felt hopeless. I said to myself, "I cannot do this! I cannot change! It's too hard!"

I was hungry and weak, so the enemy was trying to drag me back into his lies so I could sin against God, which meant to go back to being negative. This would mean living unhappily and living a life full of guilt. I did not fall into the enemy's trap, as God changed my heart and mind, so by the time I walked into my home, I had peace with myself and my son.

I walked into my home, and I was greeted by all the things that were in my living room and on dining room walls that God had given me, his revelations of writings, Bible verses, and drawings.

In the evening, my husband came to visit, so I shared with him that God had made me see that my negative thoughts were lies of the enemy that I was believing. He then shared with me that he had been wanting to see me and ask me to start again, like when we went out the first time. He had invited me to have coffee and break bread together, and after a few coffee outings, we fell in love.

After he said those words, I was brought back to when we fell in love and had the butterfly feelings. We both had lost our concept of time, sleep, and appetite. Oh, this idea of starting over again made me feel so good. I could almost feel those butterflies again. I told him that it was a good idea to start over again. He shared that he had so much love for me, but I pushed him away. The visit was short but incredibly good. We said goodbye and agreed that we would be together when we were both ready to live together and never be separated again.

In the morning, my husband had asked me via text if he could come home, if I was ready to receive him. I had longed for this moment, so I instantly texted yes but then right away realized that I was not ready. I needed to continue in this fasting and prayer for seven days.

I said, "I am not ready because God is working in me, and I need more time to work on changing."

I needed to continue with the fast so these negative thoughts and chains would be completely torn from my life. He understood. Then he shared with me that he was seeking more of God. So, God was working and healing us both. He gave me a double portion of his blessings today. The first was my victory over negative thoughts, Satan's lies, and seeing my husband and hearing about his desire for spiritual growth.

The second was that God made me see that the earth is the only place where I can have an earthly marriage, meaning a husband and wife. I can have peace knowing that it does not matter to God how many times I have been in a love relationship or how many husbands I had in the past, because to Him I am still a woman of worth. This revelation brought me freedom from guilt and shame for having so many failed relationships and marriages. The Lord God desires for me to stay focused on my earthy marriage, which is with my husband, and my marriage that counts in heaven, my marriage to the Lord Jesus Christ.

In heaven, there will be no marriage of man and woman, but we all will be like angels. And God showed it to me with these verses. Matthew 22:23–30 reads,

> The same day came to Him the Sadducees, which say that there is no resurrection, and asked Him, Saying, Master, Moses said, If a man die, having no children, his brother shall marry his wife, and raise up seed unto his brother. Now there were with us seven brethren: and the first, when he had married a wife, deceased, and, having no issue, left his wife unto his brother: Likewise the second also, and the third, unto the seventh. And last of all the woman died also. Therefore in the resurrection whose wife shall she be of the seven? for they all had her. Jesus answered and said unto them, Ye do err, not knowing the scriptures, nor the power of God. For in the resurrection they neither marry, nor are given in marriage, but are as the angels of God in heaven.

In heaven, we will all be single. There will be no husband-wife relationship. So, the only chance that I have of having a marriage is on this earth, and I want that, to love each other as husband and wife and to grow together. Now that I understand better every day what marriage is and what I want mine to be, this helps me to keep leaving my husband in God's hands. The Lord God can keep doing whatever he needs to do so we can have this earthly marriage as it should be, loving God and each other always, despite the circumstances in our lives.

It was time for dinner, so I ate fruit while my son enjoyed his dinner. We prayed together before he went to bed, and then I spent time in prayer alone, thanking God for his revelations and asking for help to not focus on negative things in my life and the lives of those around me. I asked that I may remember it is the enemy and his lies who are behind the negativity.

I thanked God so much for showing me the earthly marriage and for my husband's visit. I asked God to give me his thoughts and to use my tongue, for when the enemy strikes, I can do what it says in 2 Corinthians 10:4–6,

> For the weapons of our warfare are not carnal, but mighty through God to the pulling down of strong holds; Casting down imaginations, and every high thing that exalteth itself against the knowledge of God, and bringing into captivity every thought to the obedience of Christ; And having in a readiness to revenge all disobedience, when your obedience is fulfilled.

I prayed, asking God to bless my life, marriage, family, and the church. What I had lived before was my past. Some had been good decisions; others were bad decisions. The sins I committed against God no longer counted because I had asked Him for forgiveness, and He had forgiven me. Also, not everything was sin; some things were just bad decisions made in my immaturity.

Now the enemy could no longer bring me down and accuse me, telling me, "How can you be a believer if you have done bad things in your life?" Now I am focused on what God has shown me and I've realized that I need to use better words when speaking. I need to have a new vocabulary! My dad had told me on several occasions that when I was a little girl, a lady told him that I was going to be a great woman, but I never believed it! But no more!

Now I am focused on having good thoughts, and I believe I am a great woman! Despite all that I have been through and have suffered in my life, I've never renounced my faith in God. I have continued to fight for my life and family day after day. I have a lot to offer as a person to my sons, husband, our families, and the people in this world. I am not a great woman because of who I am but because who my God is. I have a Great GOD, and that is why I am a great woman! Proverbs 15:1 reads, "A soft answer turneth away wrath: but grievous words stir up anger" and Proverbs 21:23 says, "Whoso keepeth his mouth and his tongue keepeth his soul from troubles."

God prompted me to write a list of how far He has brought me in my life so I would see how He has used me. My oppression was so heavy that I could not see how much God had used me. I was focused on lies, but no more! It was difficult to make this list because I had never done this before, but doing it helped me to practice being focused on God. By doing so, I realized that I had had so many blessings but could not share them all. So, I had to make my list short. Praise God, I have been so blessed! This list was never for my glory but done in obedience to what God asked me to do.

With this new attitude, I could now see how great God is and what He has done in my life, my sons' lives, and my family. I could see that I have been a good instrument in the hands of God and that I have been able to bear fruit for his kingdom. Here is a summary of my life blessings and service to my King Jesus Christ.

My Blessings in My Personal Life

I am blessed to have Jesus Christ as my Lord and Savior and to be growing in my relationship with God through his Holy Spirit. I am blessed to have the freedom to worship the Lord God at home, church, and wherever I go.

I was born in a large and loving family made of my parents and ten siblings. In total, I have eleven siblings because I was blessed with a stepbrother from my father's previous marriage. Despite my stepbrother not growing and living with us, he always accepted and loved us, and so did his family. I was raised with all-natural medicine since my parents practice natural medicine. My dad was a chiropractor (*sobador*), which allowed him to always be able to care for us physically too. He always worked as self-employed and worked hard at home and outside of the home. He was a handyman. I grew up with fresh homemade food and with so many fresh fruits that we have in the Caribbean. I grew with what they call these days "organic food." Oh, and plenty of tasty bread, especially sweetbreads.

I had both parents who showed me how to work hard, how to live honestly and intensely. My mother was a hardworking woman who was always cooking, cleaning, caring, and tending to us, her eleven children. I was blessed with a mother who cooks so well and never minds cooking and feeding so many hungry mouths. I remember growing up at home and her food, how we were always waiting to eat her tasty homemade food.

That was the smell of home! She'd make flour tortillas, and as soon as she would put one on the container, a little or big hand would grab it! If you were fast, you would grab one tortilla, and if not, you would have to wait for more to be made, which would be soon. We never had a big table to sit all of us, so we had to wait turns to eat. At our table, we always had habanero chili and a container with sugar. This sugar was in case you ate too much hot pepper.

My mom would say, "Eat some sugar to stop the hot chili from burning in your mouth."

My parents taught us to live with integrity and to never be ashamed of work. My dad always said, "Never be ashamed of working, but be ashamed that instead of working, you are caught stealing."

We were raised with close family ties, which we have until this day despite having a big family. As with any family, we have disagreements, but we try to never allow them to keep us apart.

I am blessed with eight amazing brothers who are always willing to give and help the family. I remember when my older brothers had to leave home to go work in another city. They would not forget us, but they always came to visit. They would come to visit and bring lots of spare change and distribute it among us the younger kids, which were four of us. I would use this money to buy food at school, something I could never do before since we were poor. Normally I would eat at home before and after school because we could not afford to buy meals at school.

God used my brothers to spoil me while I was growing up and through the rest of my life. Each one of them has treated me out to eat or has cooked for me. They all have been there for me and my children, especially in the most difficult times in our lives. My brothers and their families are a blessing for my family and me! I am blessed with three amazing sisters. Some helped my mother care for me when I was little. My dear sisters have extended their help to me the same way as my brothers. They always helped me and supported me when I needed a place to live, food, or care for my children. My sisters constantly show me the sacrificial love that they have for their own families and the family. My sisters with their families are my blessings too.

Also, I see how I was blessed by having met my grandfather and each of my parent's family side. At a young age, my parents made sure we met them and knew who our family was. I have beautiful memories for when they would come to visit us or when we would go visit them, and they always had great food, talks, much laughter, and even some dancing. I have seen families struggle with just having a relationship with their own parents or siblings, and because of that, they lack a relationship with the extended family. I thank God that this is not the case with my family, but on the contrary, I have been blessed with this great family unity.

I experienced the blessing of God fulfilling my desire to travel and visit many countries, accompanied by my two sons. We visited Germany, Austria, Italy, Spain, Ireland, and France. Also, I have traveled with my husband, and it has been such a blessing to enjoy this different season of my life with him. I am blessed with knowing how to drive and the privilege of having to drive in different countries. From my young age and until my young adult days, I had to walk to school, work, and church when I was back home. I'd walk because I did not have money to pay for my bus fare, so I would have to walk short or long distances in an extremely hot climate. For more than twenty years, I have been blessed with a vehicle, so I did not need to take a bus or walk unless I wanted to.

I had always desired to get a degree, but due to my poverty, my parents could not afford it. Nor could I. God blessed me by giving me the endurance and provision so I could finish a degree in my mid-forties. I now have my Associate's Degree in Science of Human Services from Columbia College of Missouri. I have been given the ability to be able to speak, write, and understand two languages, Spanish and English.

I have been able to bear children. Being a mother is a privilege and blessing from God. God had blessed me with two great sons, and I have been able to raise them. I am grateful for having sons who are very loving and forgiving. They constantly show me God's love. I am blessed with a great bond with both of my sons and the privilege that they trust me to help them when in need of direction or help in life. I am blessed that I have sons who have a loving heart for God, family, and others. I have been blessed to see God's blessing and favor toward my children and me. Because of my sons, I learned how to pray and not to give up in life. They constantly teach me how to love unconditionally. I had the privilege of being a stepmother and helped raise two great kids. I was blessed to be in their lives and share our lives together.

It was such a blessing to raise these four kids and enjoy all the adventures that we had as a family from picnics to trip to the park and vacations. I was thankful for all the love I received from them and for loving them back. It was so much that I learned by being a mother and stepmother, and that was a blessing. I am blessed that my husband is a father too, that he is blessed with two adult sons and that he comes from a large family too. Another important family for me is my friends and their families. God had blessed me with seeing the importance of cultivating this friendship bond and cherishing them. I am so blessed to have them in my life. I thank God that he has blessed me with these great love bonds of family and friends.

I was blessed by being at my dad's side in the last three hours before his death. I was able to fly from San Diego to Southern Mexico and made it in time to say goodbye to my father. I sat on a small stool right by his feet at his bed and spent an hour reading the Bible to him. Then my father no longer wanted to be laying down but wanted to sit down in the bed, so he sat down. Now he was facing me and looked at me, and it seemed as if he wanted to say something. I was still sitting down on my stool, and standing next to me were three other siblings, one sister and two brothers.

I encouraged my dad to say goodbye to us and to let God know that he was ready to go home, ready for heaven. After saying this to my father, he dropped two tears. Two tears rolled down his cheeks and fell on his lap since he was sitting down. This was a miracle because cancer had taken away his ability to produce any tears or cry, but God gave him these tears to say goodbye to us, his family. Moments later my father lay down in his bed. Then I asked my brother, the pastor, to join me at my dad's bed to pray for the Lord to take him home. The two of us are the youngest of the kids.

My dad had always loved and feared God, but a year before his sickness, he accepted Jesus Christ as his Savior, and now he had a personal relationship with Him. I knelt on my dad's bed by his shoulder. I put my right hand on his chest and my left hand holding his right hand, and I started to pray. Before I prayed, I dedicated him a song and played it. This was a song that was being sung from a daughter to her father, thanking her father for what he had done for her.

While the song was playing, I was praying for God to take him home since he was ready and for him to die peacefully. I finished my prayer at the same time as the song. After I said amen, I opened my eyes and saw my dad take his last breath very peacefully and die. What a blessing to be at my father's side and see his last breath, knowing he is going to be with JESUS, face-to-face! My father was able to live for 87 years on earth, but now he lives for eternity in heaven!

In 2015, I was blessed by finally being able to swim underwater in Cancun. I couldn't go swimming underwater before because of my close drowning experience as a child. I grew up attending church events at the beach in Campeche and Cancun. They were both cities by the ocean, but I did not swim and would just stand in the shallow part of the water. I tried snorkeling only twice in my life, when I was sixteen years old, but I couldn't because I panicked. On my honeymoon, I held my husband's hand and trusted him, and I let him lead me underwater for the whole time we were given in the tour, which was around thirty minutes. I got to see the fish and more underwater. Now I know why people get so excited about snorkeling in Cancun. It was amazing!

I can recognize what a blessing my husband is to me, despite not being with him now. I thank God that for the first time in my life, I had all the steps of a love relationship—the courtship, dating, engagement, and then wedding. At the civil wedding, I had both of my sons and a small group of friends. I was blessed that for the first time in my life, I had my family attend my wedding, a desire fulfilled. My mother and most of my siblings were at my wedding. The religious wedding was at a secluded beautiful hacienda (estate) back home with my mother, some siblings and family, great food, and mariachi music! It was a dream wedding! I wanted a Mexican wedding and have my family with me, and God granted my desire. Thank you, God!

My Blessings in My Ministry

I have the blessing of starting to serve God at a young age in the ministry that He has given me. I started the mission work at the age of fifteen and did it for a few years and then stopped, but resumed at the age of twenty-four, totaling twenty-two years of service to God. I served in Mexico in the following cities: Campeche, Merida, Tijuana, Tecate, Rosarito, and Cabo San Lucas. In the United States, I served in San Diego, Oceanside, Vista, and Missouri. I have been able to do mission work using two languages, English and Spanish. I directed a nonprofit in Oceanside, California, and opened a nonprofit in Mexico.

In my home, I started a food ministry *"God's Warehouse"* and accepted miscellaneous donations, which I drove to Tijuana three times a week to be distributed in the community, pastors, missionaries, Christian seminary, senior home, orphanages, and other cities of Mexico. I directed and ran monthly mission trips to Tijuana where we had outreaches for the community and cooked for many of these events with the help of others. I distributed monthly donations to families in my city too from my food bank at home. I am blessed to know that this food ministry continues at my local church, where they continue to help families in need.

I am blessed to be part of the mission work for so many years in collaboration with other servants where I helped by coordinating and participating in outreaches for women, children, and youth in Mexico. I helped other ministries by translating in various outreaches in Mexico. I served in prayer and intercessory prayer, advocating for those who were sick, poor, or in need. I participated in hurricane relief outreach in Cabo San Lucas and helped the Haitian refugees in Tijuana. I organized and directed a fundraising concert for missions and taught women's Bible classes on the military base and at home in Missouri.

Through all the years of mission work, I have been able to see lives transformed besides mine and my family, including those whom I served and those who were serving in the ministry. I have seen some servants become pastors, missionaries, and Christians on fire for the Lord. In Tijuana, two of the youth who served with us joined the seminary, and here in Oceanside, one became a pastor.

All this missionary work has been possible, thanks to God who first called me and then provided. I am truly blessed that He had chosen me to do this extensive mission work. I had no idea that when God called me as a teenager, I would be taken to another country so I could get the resources to help my country of Mexico and fulfill my calling as a leader on the mission work. This leadership calling would be fulfilled in the other country too, where I got to use the same resources to help families in need in Oceanside and the surrounding areas. All glory to God! Also, thanks to my family, friends, churches, neighbors, and businesses who donated for the missionary work. Without them, all this mission work could have never been possible. Thank God for all the servants from the United States who served in this ministry. You made it possible to be able to reach more people for Christ. I have been blessed to have served with you and all the memories we get to have for working for Christ and loving on his people in the mission field.

I thank God for using my brother, Jose Luis, to take me on my first visit to the missions and for providing me with my younger brother and partner for all this missionary work for so many years, my brother, Pastor Angel. His family and the church in Tijuana served with us and gave us all their love too. I am thankful for all the ministries we got to partner with and help in Tijuana and other cities and for all the pastors and missionaries I met through this ministry. I thank the orphanage in Playas de Tijuana who has made a major impact in my life. The staff and children are so dear to my heart. I am blessed to serve among so many servants and that they had allowed me to be part of their life. They have made a big impact in my life that I would never be the same but seek to serve as they serve, with that sacrificial love of Christ.

I finished this list in awe of how much God has done through my life, a small and imperfect woman. But only God could use an imperfect woman like me to do his perfect and amazing work! God is faithful! I am his daughter, and he has used me and will keep using me and my family for his honor and glory! Hallelujah! I give glory to God for allowing me to have lived this long and see all his blessings in my personal life, the ministry, and my calling! Thank you, GOD. You are Great!

Chapter 6

ENEMY'S OPPRESSION AND MY FAITH IN GOD

The Spirit of the Lord God is upon me; because the Lord hath anointed me to preach good tidings unto the meek; He hath sent me to bind up the brokenhearted, to proclaim liberty to the captives, and the opening of the prison to them that are bound; To proclaim the acceptable year of the Lord, and the day of vengeance of our God; to comfort all that mourn; To appoint unto them that mourn in Zion, to give unto them beauty for ashes, the oil of joy for mourning, the garment of praise for the spirit of heaviness; that they might be called trees of righteousness, the planting of the Lord, that He might be glorified.

—Isaiah 61:1–3

Day 6 out of 7. Is Tuesday, my morning went as usual. I took my son to school and returned home. When I got home, I sat in my dining room to eat my fast portion. My kitchen is one of my favorite places in my home because that is the place where I cook the physical food for my family. I love taking care of them, and cooking is one of the ways I can show them my love. My other favorite place is my dining table, where I receive the physical food but also the spiritual one. Here at this table is where I spend most of my time with God in prayer, gratitude, praise, cries, and questions. Also here is where He speaks to me, dazzles me, and reveals his Word, knowledge, wisdom, love, and mercy. And here is where I find peace, joy, order, and purpose. This is the only way I can be obedient by spending time with Jesus Christ.

The Lord reminded me today of my purpose. Yes, God said to me, "Delilah, do you remember what I called you for?"

I answered, "Yes, Lord, of course I remember!"

I started to recall when I was sixteen and received my calling, although at that time I didn't know that's what just happened, and it took me years to know it. This was the time when I was living at my brother's home with his wife and attending church with them. My Nazarene church in Campeche was having a revival service, and the invited worship group was playing. When they did the altar call, I went to pray as I felt God calling me. I was already saved and baptized so I did not go to the altar for that. I just felt that God was saying that I needed to serve him. I did not understand what he meant because I was already serving in a ministry at the church and passionate about serving him and the missionary work.

I did not know what to do after I went to the altar. Was I supposed to join a Christian seminary? I did not feel that I needed to join a seminary, but that I needed to be a helper to the missions field. But I did not know what that meant. So, I did what I could, and with my brother, I visited missions whenever possible. I never spoke with anyone about how I felt, and I could not explain how I felt anyway. I was just a young teenager who had a hunger for living an abundant life in Christ.

At this same age, I had another experience with God, and this happened while living with my brother and his wife. One day I was watching a TV program that was showing African countries with so many needs and in poverty that I started to cry. During this TV program, I felt the burden and need to help those in vulnerable situations and much need. I had never felt this way until that time. I grew up in poverty and was still poor, so seeing disadvantaged people was common to me, but this was the first time I reacted to this. It was because this would be my calling, although I did not know it at the time.

My brother, Jose Luis, asked me, "Why are you crying?"

I shared with him that it was because of what I had just seen on TV about the destitute children with their families in Africa, how I wanted to help, but I was disadvantaged too so I could not do anything to help them.

My brother changed from being concerned to joy and then said to me, "Delilah, it is the Holy Spirit who touched you and made you feel this way."

That was the end of that experience on that day. I did not know what else I should do. Since that day I have always wanted to go to Africa to visit and share how God used their country to give my calling. This same brother was the one who took me on missionary trips probably because he saw my heart, and he became my spiritual father.

Due to my move to Tijuana, I lost the influence of my brother in my life but thank God that he had my younger brother who would come to study to be a pastor in Tecate, a close distance to Tijuana. While he was studying at the seminary, we started the mission work together and have been working together ever since through all these years. This is not a coincidence but God's divine plan.

After I was done remembering how God called me and the ways He used to go about it, the Lord led me to read and meditate on Isaiah 61:1–3.

> The Spirit of the Lord God is upon me; because the Lord hath anointed me to preach good tidings unto the meek; he hath sent me to bind up the brokenhearted, to proclaim liberty to the captives, and the opening of the prison to them that are bound; To proclaim the acceptable year of the Lord, and the day of vengeance of our God; to comfort all that mourn; To appoint unto them that mourn in Zion, to give unto them beauty for ashes, the oil of joy for mourning, the garment of praise for the spirit of

heaviness; that they might be called trees of righteousness,
the planting of the Lord, that He might be glorified.

Then under his direction, I placed on my living room walls the revelations I had received from Him since I lived in Germany and all the way until today. Before I taped anything on the walls, my communication with God was so open that it flowed both ways. It was glorious to have Him speak to me! I then worshiped Him through songs and prayers. I was savoring Jesus, the lover of my soul. Then I started declaring God's purpose in my life through a worship song that became my prayer.

By the time I played the second song, I could finally believe in my calling. My calling was not lost, but I had only passed through the valley of the shadow of death and God's purifying fire. I realized that for almost a year I had lived as a defeated warrior because Satan had me oppressed and I had become captive with strongholds. I, Delilah, had believed his lies, and little by little I was ceasing to believe in the truth the Bible, the Word of God, in his promises and my calling!

The enemy had oppressed me through my weaknesses, my mind and food. I was believing lies, thinking negative thoughts, and eating certain foods that caused me to feel depressed and have bad allergic reactions in my body. I had fallen into lies. My spirit and flesh were wrestling. And these demons who were looking for my death were frightening me, and I did not even know it! So now I understand why God told me last Wednesday that these demons only leave with fasting and prayer! I never would have thought and much less realized that subtly the enemy of my soul was stomping all over me!

When thinking about fasting, I had only seen the reason as praying for my marriage and sons. I never thought that this was what God would reveal to me, that I was not preaching life in Jesus Christ, but I was living my life halfway. Had it not been for this fasting and praying, I would have never realized it since the enemy of our soul works so subtly and always uses lies. And like a fool I was believing it!

God reminds me who the enemy is in John 8:44, "Ye are of your father the devil, and the lusts of your father ye will do. He was a murderer from the beginning, and abode not in the truth, because there is no truth in him. When he speaketh a lie, he speaketh of his own: for he is a liar, and the father of it."

With God's revelation now, I can keep moving, and with the power of the Holy Spirit, I rebuked Satan and his demons! Thank God for his deliverance in my life! Death no longer lurks in my life, but I have life in Jesus Christ! Now I fully believe in every verse of the Bible, and now I am ready! I am a warrior of Jesus Christ! I prayed with each song declaring with my mouth, saying, "I, Delilah, declare God said blessed be the name of the Lord Jesus Christ. Blessed is my life, my family, the church, and the world."

While playing a song, I was able to remember the time when I was living in Missouri and had asked God to see his glory and bring Him glory. After this thought, I could hear God telling me, "Today you have brought me glory, and you have seen my glory. But cling to ME, and you will continue to bring me glory. You will see my glory, the one you yearn for, to See ME Face-to-Face! I will come for you, Delilah."

I am unable to explain how I felt after this experience with God, but you will understand it when you experience God in your life in this way.

Over a year ago, it was very engraved in my heart to want to have the faith of Abraham. Then with this last Thursday teaching in chapter 1 called "Today You Exist!" I was able to understand what it means when the Bible says that Abraham believed, and he was counted for righteous.

Today, I prayed, "Lord Jesus, I believe, and now I have the faith that Abraham had, and I declare it in my life, my family, and the church" Now I could say, "Delilah, your faith has been counted to you for righteousness." And I know it is God who tells me this in Hebrews 11:8, "By faith Abraham (Delilah), when he (she) was called to go out into a place which he (she) should after receive for an inheritance, obeyed; and he (she) went out, not knowing whither he (she) went."

After I read this verse, I continued in a gratitude prayer, thanking God for giving me faith like Abraham, a faith that believes in God alone and that it is not moved no matter what has happened or is happening around me. I know it is not going to be easy, but I must keep my faith in God and keep growing in Him. I am ready with my marching orders for the service of my King JESUS CHRIST!

God gave me these verses to encourage me: Psalm 108:13; 1 John 3:8;

Joshua 1:5; Isaiah 40:31; 54:17, 61:11; Deuteronomy 11:25; Hebrews 4:12; 2 Samuel 22:35; Ephesians 6:17; and Esther 4:16. I no longer focus on being negative, but I am focused on life, my life through JESUS CHRIST! I now speak of life and God's blessings in my life. All that God showed me from the first day of fasting and until today I had put it on my walls. I could see how everything was arranged to fall in place, and it was no coincidence but a divine plan. God is wonderful. He patiently waited for me to understand what was happening in my life.

Tonight at 6:30 p.m., I took my son to the youth service and then returned home. When I opened the door, I heard God telling me, "Now, Delilah, I want you to meditate. Do not turn on the music. Do not write. But meditate. Just meditate."

So, I sat on one side of my couch and prayed that I would quiet my mind and be in silence. I finally shut down my mind after a few minutes and was able to meditate on God. I discovered that God was surrounding me all over in my home through his Word. In my kitchen, I had a picture based on this verse, Matthew 11:28–30, "Come unto me, all ye that labour and are heavy laden, and I will give you rest. Take my yoke upon you and learn of me; for I am meek and lowly in heart: and ye shall find rest unto your souls. For my yoke is easy, and my burden is light."

After meditating on this, I got up and sat on the other side of my couch. As I looked up, I could realize that the Bible verse in my kitchen had come true in my life. I have had the peace of Christ as I have passed through the fire and the shadow of the valley of death. Today, despite not having my husband at home and knowing that soon I will no longer have a home to live in, I have peace. Even though my sons will need money for college and have other needs, I have peace. Although I am hungry and with many blisters in my mouth due to accidental bites today while eating, I have peace. Despite all this, I am not alone because I have GOD and my family. I am trusting that GOD the Great King holds his daughter in his hands! I am in the palm of his hands, and I am the apple of his eyes! Hallelujah!

Though I have been afflicted, He has been my salvation, and that is of human nature what I had gone through. God had given me the strength to endure it all and the faith to be able to trust Him. He has been my answer and my way! The Lord God gave me these two verses:

Psalm 42:5 reads, "Why art thou cast down, O my soul? and why art thou disquieted in me? hope thou in God: for I shall yet praise Him for the help of his countenance."

1 Corinthians 10:13 states, "There hath no temptation taken you but such as is common to man: but God is faithful, who will not suffer you to be tempted above that ye are able; but will with the temptation also make a way to escape, that ye may be able to bear it."

Looking at my walls, I see my wall of faith. For a few years, I had been wanting to put a wall of faith in my living room as part of my wall decorations, but never got to do it. When I thought about doing the wall of faith, I did not have it planned this way though. My idea was to put pictures of my father and grandfather as well as their testimonies with Bible verses. This was going to be about my family lineage. They are great testimonies of faith, love, and courage. But today as I was putting all that God instructed me to put on the walls, I could see that this wall of faith was about God and Delilah, although I haven't finished it yet.

When I realized this revelation, I had to play a worship song that talks about how God dances around us while we are unaware, and that is how I felt. Yes, God's presence has always been with me without me noticing it so many times. Now the Lord leads me to read Zephaniah 3:17, "The Lord thy God in the midst of thee is mighty; He will save, He will rejoice over thee with joy; He will rest in his love, He will joy over thee with singing."

I then picked up my son from church and returned home. I prayed with my son, and he went to sleep. Meanwhile I stayed awake and continued to meditate on my wall, on how it is about Delilah's life. On this wall are included people and countries where I have lived before, including where I am today. As a person, I am not alone in this world, but I am part of God's plan that goes beyond my plan. I understand now. I laughed in joy and awe! God has been wanting me to stay focused on him and me to be married to him. This is the vision he gave me a few years ago, the one called "The Cross" is image 2 in chapter 1, which shows how the relationship should look like. A marriage is what Jesus Christ asked me to have with Him. I struggled on having that type of relationship with Him, of having a marriage with Jesus, but now I understand it, and I am willing to have it! This whole wall is all about DELILAH because it is DELILAH'S testimony! I can share with people about my family heritage, but the only thing I need to focus on is my relationship with God and my life, on how DELILAH lives for GOD!

It is 11:13 p.m. I cannot and do not want to fall asleep as I long for God to keep revealing Himself to me. When I am not fasting, I go to bed around this time, but due to my fasting, I have been going to bed around 9:00 p.m. because I feel a little weak and hungry, but not tonight. I asked the Lord Jesus to manifest Himself in my weakness and give me the strength to write what He shows me. I have been wanting to attend a prayer vigil. As a youth, I attended so many, and I loved them and missed them. And tonight, I heard God telling me, "My daughter, you wanted a prayer vigil night. Well, here you have it! Stay awake, listen to Me, and wait on Me!"

So, I ate some fruit after this encounter with God and continued with this vigil night. The Lord reveals to me that I have just experienced a revival in my life through this fasting and praying. I had to experience revival in my life first. Then God could use me to bring revival. Now I could sit down and with clarity of mind write what He has done, doing, and is going to do in my life. Hallelujah! Amen! To God be the glory forever and ever. Amen! Thank God that He manifests Himself in my life and answers the petitions of my heart. It is 12:08 a.m., and before I go to sleep, God gave me a writing called "The Shower."

The Shower

For the weapons of our warfare are not carnal, but mighty through God to the pulling down of strong holds; Casting down imaginations, and every high thing that exalteth itself against the knowledge of God and bringing into captivity every thought to the obedience of Christ; And having in a readiness to revenge all disobedience, when your obedience is fulfilled.
—2 Corinthians 10:4–6

Your body gets dirty every day, so you need to take a shower to clean yourself. It does not matter which type of shower or bathtub you may have. What matters is that you clean up yourself every day. But there is a problem because you are bathing in your shower that still has its stopper and all the dirty water that has been accumulated from days past. You choose to not remove the stopper, so the dirty water is not going out. So, it does not matter how much water falls on top of your body. You are still dirty. Yes, you are still dirty because your feet stand in all the dirty water that you have accumulated for days or years. Through this study, God shows me how the old Delilah used to be, but now how I can live my daily life in Christ.

- **Water from the Shower:** The Word of God (The Bible)
- **Tub:** Your mind or your beliefs
- **Dirty Water:** What you live in your daily life
- **Stopper:** What you do not want to let go of or change

As a Christian, you hear and may read the Word of God, the Bible, but you are not believing it. But instead, you believe other things. So therefore, you find yourself collecting in your tub the dirty water of all the baths you have taken in your life, which is causing you to still be walking with dirty feet.

Do not do that anymore! Take the stopper off the tub and rinse the tub. Let clean water bathe you only. Use the stopper! The stopper of the tub has a purpose, to hold the clean water and to empty the water once is dirty. Use your stopper for what it was created to be, and this is the only way you can get out of the bathroom clean. From now on, the only water that your body should receive every time you bathe should be only from the shower because you are now emptying the dirty water from your tub daily. This shower has washed away every bit of dirt from your body, so now you are completely clean. No more halfway showers! Let your life be cleaned daily with the Word of God, the Bible, and live believing, standing, and walking in it! Remember, God has chosen you to be a head and not a tail, so walk like it! You are victorious in JESUS CHRIST! God loves you. He paid a great price for you at the cross, so walk in victory!

Chapter 7

THE BRIDE AND THE GROOM

PART ONE

WHO IS THE BRIDE?

Day 7 out of 7. Is Wednesday, is my last day of fasting. Thank God I did it! I was on my seventh day. As usual, I took my son to school and then returned home. As I seek God this morning, he revealed more reasons for why I had to fast for seven days. I could now understand the meaning of the number seven that the Lord gave me on my vision in April 2014 when I had fasted for five days. As I reflected on these seven days, I saw that again God has given me the number seven.

I am now staring at the side of my dining room wall, and I see seven Bible verses. This was the first wall where God led me to hang verses. But it is not just about the number seven, but the meaning of it, of what God accomplished in these seven days in my life. These walls in my home displayed God's revelations, plans, and purpose for my life. The Lord had been speaking to me through the Holy Spirit and his Son Jesus Christ. Now I clearly understand it. This is what they called to be completed by the Holy Spirit, the fullness of Christ. I could now serve God and fulfill my purpose in life and bring glory to God. I see how God has always been present in my life during battles and victories. Hallelujah!

For many years, I had desired to have my house as a house of prayer like the Bible says in Matthew 21:13, "And said unto them, It is written, My house shall be called the house of prayer." I desire that every person who enters my house receives peace and encouragement to continue walking with the Lord Jesus Christ. And if they do not know Jesus Christ, let them receive Him and leave my home blessed with peace and encouragement.

As they enter my home, they will see my wall of faith, my life testimony, and be encouraged to continue walking in faith with Jesus Christ no matter what their circumstances are. I understand now that I am that house of prayer, that my life and testimony are what people can see and be encouraged by.

I am so thankful that I have fallen into the merciful hands of my God, just like King David from the Bible. This causes me to laugh and weep with joy. When King David was confronted about his sin with Bathsheba and for killing her husband, he was given three choices from which he would need to pick one to receive his punishment. One option was God, what David chose. He did not want to choose a man's punishment because he knew how a man could be cruel and evil. So, he chose God's punishment, knowing that God was going to be merciful with him. God has lifted my fallen hands and lifted my head and filled my glass to overflowing!

Who Is the Bride? Delilah, The Body of Christ, The Church

The Day I Became the Bride: Day of Salvation October 1983

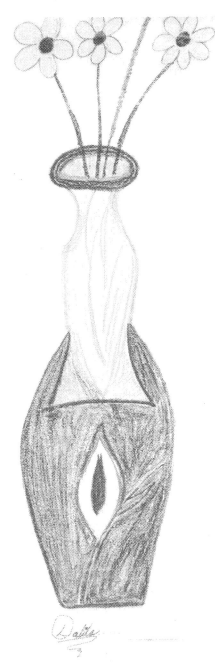

In 2016 and a few months into my marriage, I drew on a piece of paper that I had recycled from an old calendar. I was at home sitting down in the living room when I started to stare at a small flowerpot with flowers that my husband had given me. I had placed them on top of a big empty flowerpot that I had gotten from the thrift shop of an orphanage in Tijuana. I got up and went to get a piece of paper to write. I grabbed the first piece of paper I found that was available for me, my old calendar. This sheet is ripped on one side and written on the back, but the other side used to be blank until I used it to do this drawing. I drew a large vase with a flower bouquet inside. This bouquet of flowers is missing a flower, and instead it has only a stalk. If you were to look at it, you could say it is pretty. You may also say that I should have used a new blank paper and thrown away this one in the trash since it had already been used. However, this is not the case because I still found a use for it just as is.

Today through my flower vase drawing, God made me see that this drawing represents me, Delilah the bride. I am a bride who has suffered, been broken into pieces, and remains incomplete. I have been recycled by God and for God! When I thought my life was meaningless and over, God turned my life around, just like the recycled paper. The back still had a use, so my life still has a purpose! I am still Jesus's bride! So just as this vase is beautiful, so I am beautiful for God. I can be used to put flowers in my vase and brighten someone's life when they meet me or look at me.

Every person in this world will have problems and sufferings, but that is not the only thing that matters in our life. What matters is that we have the hope that one day we will be in heaven with God and have no more sufferings and pain. Meantime while we are on earth, we are a bride waiting for her Groom, waiting to meet JESUS CHRIST Face-to-Face!

God makes me see that I am supposed to be incomplete on this earth, just like that vase is incomplete because it is missing a flower. Well, I am incomplete too because I am missing my groom, Jesus Christ. I need to remember that I am beautiful to God and that I will become whole once I meet JESUS Face-to-Face, so meantime on earth, I need to keep living complete, which is only through his Holy Spirit. The Lord gives me the same Bible verse that I started my day with yesterday, Isaiah 61:1–3.

The Spirit of the Lord God is upon me; because the Lord hath anointed me to preach good tidings unto the meek; he hath sent me to bind up the brokenhearted, to proclaim liberty to the captives, and the opening of the prison to them that are bound; To proclaim the acceptable year of the Lord, and the day of vengeance of our God; to comfort all that mourn; To appoint unto them that mourn in Zion, to give unto them beauty for ashes, the oil of joy for mourning, the garment of praise for the spirit of heaviness; that they might be called trees of righteousness, the planting of the Lord, that He might be glorified.

As part of this process of God, I had to learn how I was created and why this way.

Personalities

I love that God created us with different personalities that can be used to teach us how to love one another despite our differences. Sometimes our personalities may even clash with others because we are remarkably similar, and that is not bad, but it can be challenging. For example, one of my sons has a similar personality to mine. We are both extroverts, energetic and talkers. Oftentimes the similarity in personality benefits our relationships because it helps us agree since we could see things the same way. On the other hand, on some occasions, we could not agree, and that is when our personalities will clash. Being aware of our personalities difference has helped me to not hold things against my son or others but to exercise self-control and be more patience. I must keep trusting God that my personality has a great purpose in my calling and that he is still working in me, just like he is working in my family and those around me. Thank God that He made us with different personalities so we could work together on making this world a better place, which can only be done through God's love.

Talents or Abilities

We all have different talents (abilities) that we have inherited from our parents. For example, I have a manual ability. I can use my hands to cook from basic to more complicated cooking, like making fresh breads, tortillas, or other baked goods or meals. I have used this talent very much during my years serving God and others. Most of the cooking I done, I have learned on my own, so I consider myself a natural cook. I make my own recipes and enjoy cooking very much. I inherited the talent of cooking from my maternal grandfather. My mother's father loved to cook, my mother loves to cook, and I love to cook too. So, this ability of cooking I inherited from my family.

Another example is the social ability I inherited from my family. Both of my parents were talkers and made friends easily. Both of my maternal grandparents had the ability to communicate with people too. So now you know why I am a talker because it is "a family thing." My mother tells me the story that before my grandfather married my grandmother, he lived and worked as a chef for twelve years at a Catholic priest convent. He was a very peaceful person, but he also enjoyed talking. My grandmother did what was not common in those days. She went to college to study and learn about the laws, and she used her social ability to defend the poor and needy. My grandfather met her at the college, and then they married. They had a small grocery store at home, which my grandfather and the daughters normally attended. Also, my grandfather mostly ran the home since my grandmother was dedicated to help those in need.

My mother tells me that many times her mother would drop off people at their home so they would care for them with food and shelter while her mother went away to fight for their rights. That is how my mother learned how to cook for a large family because many times my grandfather had to cook big pots of food to feed his family and the people that my grandmother had dropped off. This helped my mother learn how to cook and make it last for many people, which helped when she married my dad and had to feed her family size of thirteen. (It's amazing what God's plans are. What we learn in life never gets wasted but has a purpose.)

I never met my grandmother since she died many years before I was born, but a street carries her name. Thank God I did have the blessing of meeting my grandfather, who was well-known as Don Angelito, "Mr. Little Angel." He was known for his love for God and others and being a peaceful man.

Around four years ago was when I learned the story of my grandparents. It was when my mother came to visit in California. During her visit, she helped me cook a Christmas feast that I was making to take to a Christian seminary in Tecate, Mexico, to celebrate Christmas with them. I took the feast and other donations, accompanied by my mother and a friend, and we met my brother, the pastor, at the seminary. This was the first time that my mother would do a mission trip with us, her children. At the end of the outreach, my mother shared with us that this outreach brought her childhood memories of her parents using their talents to help others. It was beautiful to find out about some of the stories of my mother and grandparents.

Well, as you can see, I was able to show you examples of two great talents I inherited from my family, being a social person and the passion for cooking, both of which have been well-used in the mission field, starting with my home. So, a talent is something you are born with and inherited from your family. Do you know which talents you have?

The Body of Christ: Ministries, Callings, and Gifts of the Holy Spirit

As every man hath received the gift, even so minister the same
one to another, as good stewards of the manifold grace of God.
—1 Peter 4:10

So, we learned that the talents (abilities) are inherited from our family, and we are born with them. On the other hand, the gifts, ministries, and callings are God-given, not something you can inherit from your family. God has placed a calling on you and given you a ministry to work under and gifts from the Holy Spirit so you so can fulfill his plans and purpose for your life and bring him glory.

Diversity of Operations (Ministries): Total of Nine Ministries

Now concerning spiritual gifts, brethren, I would not have you
ignorant. Ye know that ye were Gentiles, carried away unto these
dumb idols, even as ye were led. Wherefore I give you to understand,
that no man speaking by the Spirit of God calleth Jesus accursed: and
that no man can say that Jesus is the Lord, but by the Holy Ghost.
Now there are diversities of gifts, but the same Spirit. And there are
differences of administrations, but the same Lord. And there are
diversities of operations, but it is the same God which worketh all
in all. But the manifestation of the Spirit is given to every man to
profit withal. For to one is given by the Spirit the *word of wisdom*; to
another the *word of knowledge* by the same Spirit; To another *faith*
by the same Spirit; to another the gifts of *healing* by the same Spirit;
To another the *working of miracles*; to another *prophecy*; to another
discerning of spirits; to another *divers kinds of tongues*; to another
the *interpretation of tongues*: But all these worketh that one and
the selfsame Spirit, dividing to every man severally as he will. For
as the body is one, and hath many members, and all the members
of that one body, being many, are one body: so also, is Christ.
—1 Corinthians 12:1–12 (emphasis added)

Diversity of Callings: Total of Five Calling

And He gave some, *apostles*; and some, *prophets*; and some, *evangelists*;
and some, *pastors* and *teachers*; For the perfecting of the saints, for the
work of the ministry, for the edifying of the body of Christ: Till we
all come in the unity of the faith, and of the knowledge of the Son
of God, unto a perfect man, unto the measure of the stature of the
fulness of Christ: that we henceforth be no more children, tossed to
and fro, and carried about with every wind of doctrine, by the sleight
of men, and cunning craftiness, whereby they lie in wait to deceive;
But speaking the truth in love, may grow up into him in all things,
which is the head, even Christ: From whom the whole body fitly
joined together and compacted by that which every joint supplieth,

according to the effectual working in the measure of every part,
maketh increase of the body unto the edifying of itself in Love.
—Ephesians 4:11–16 (emphasis added)

Diversity of Gifts: Total of Seven Gifts

Having then gifts differing according to the grace that is given to
us, whether *prophecy*, let us prophesy according to the proportion
of faith; Or *ministry*, let us wait on our ministering: or he that
teacheth, on teaching; Or he that *exhorteth*, on exhortation: he that
giveth, let him do it with simplicity; he that *ruleth*, with diligence;
he that *sheweth mercy*, with cheerfulness. Let love be without
dissimulation. Abhor that which is evil; cleave to that which is good.
—Romans 12:6–9 (emphasis added)

The Holy Spirit gives me these verses:

- "And all thy children shall be taught of the Lord; and great shall
  be the peace of thy children" (Isaiah 54:13).
- "Called of God an high priest after the order of Melchisedec.
  Of whom we have many things to say, and hard to be uttered,
  seeing ye are dull of hearing. For when for the time ye ought to be
  teachers, ye have need that one teach you again which be the first
  principles of the oracles of God; and are become such as have need
  of milk, and not of strong meat. For every one that useth milk is
  unskilful in the word of righteousness: for he is a babe. But strong
  meat belongeth to them that are of full age, even those who by
  reason of use have their senses exercised to discern both good and
  evil" (Hebrews 5:10–14).
- "The words of king Lemuel, the prophecy that his mother taught
  him. What, my son? and what, the son of my womb? and what,
  the son of my vows? Give not thy strength unto women, nor thy
  ways to that which destroyeth kings. It is not for kings, O Lemuel,
  it is not for kings to drink wine; nor for princes strong drink: Lest
  they drink, and forget the law, and pervert the judgment of any of
  the afflicted. Give strong drink unto him that is ready to perish,

and wine unto those that be of heavy hearts. Let him drink, and forget his poverty, and remember his misery no more. Open thy mouth for the dumb in the cause of all such as are appointed to destruction. Open thy mouth, judge righteously, and plead the cause of the poor and needy. Who can find a virtuous woman? for her price is far above rubies. The heart of her husband doth safely trust in her, so that he shall have no need of spoil. She will do him good and not evil all the days of her life. She seeketh wool, and flax, and worketh willingly with her hands. She is like the merchants' ships; she bringeth her food from afar. She riseth also while it is yet night, and giveth meat to her household, and a portion to her maidens. She considereth a field, and buyeth it: with the fruit of her hands she planteth a vineyard. She girdeth her loins with strength, and strengtheneth her arms. She perceiveth that her merchandise is good: her candle goeth not out by night. She layeth her hands to the spindle, and her hands hold the distaff. She stretcheth out her hand to the poor; yea, she reacheth forth her hands to the needy. She is not afraid of the snow for her household: for all her household are clothed with scarlet. She maketh herself coverings of tapestry; her clothing is silk and purple. Her husband is known in the gates, when he sitteth among the elders of the land. She maketh fine linen, and selleth it; and delivereth girdles unto the merchant. Strength and honour are her clothing; and she shall rejoice in time to come. She openeth her mouth with wisdom; and in her tongue is the law of kindness. She looketh well to the ways of her household, and eateth not the bread of idleness. Her children arise up, and call her blessed; her husband also, and he praiseth her. Many daughters have done virtuously, but thou excellest them all. Favour is deceitful, and beauty is vain: but a woman that feareth the Lord, she shall be praised. Give her of the fruit of her hands; and let her own works praise her in the gates" (Proverbs 31:1–31).

- "Then said Jesus unto his disciples, If any man will come after me, let him deny himself, and take up his cross, and follow me" (Matthew 16:24).

Delilah P.I.O.

The Holy Spirit now gives me these verses specifically for Israel the Remnant.

Israel the Remnant

- "I have set watchmen upon thy walls, O Jerusalem, which shall never hold their peace day nor night: ye that make mention of the Lord, keep not silence" (Isaiah 62:6a).
- "And they shall build the old wastes, they shall raise up the former desolations, and they shall repair the waste cities, the desolations of many generations. And strangers shall stand and feed your flocks, and the sons of the alien shall be your plowmen and your vinedressers. But ye shall be named the Priests of the Lord: men shall call you the Ministers of our God: ye shall eat the riches of the Gentiles, and in their glory shall ye boast yourselves. For your shame ye shall have double; and for confusion they shall rejoice in their portion: therefore in their land they shall possess the double: everlasting joy shall be unto them. For I the Lord love judgment, I hate robbery for burnt offering; and I will direct their work in truth, and I will make an everlasting covenant with them. And their seed shall be known among the Gentiles, and their offspring among the people: all that see them shall acknowledge them, that they are the seed which the Lord hath blessed. I will greatly rejoice in the Lord, my soul shall be joyful in my God; for he hath clothed me with the garments of salvation, he hath covered me with the robe of righteousness, as a bridegroom decketh himself with ornaments, and as a bride adorneth herself with her jewels. For as the earth bringeth forth her bud, and as the garden causeth the things that are sown in it to spring forth; so the Lord God will cause righteousness and praise to spring forth before all the nations" (Isaiah 61:411).
- "But the fruit of the Spirit is love, joy, peace, longsuffering, gentleness, goodness, faith, meekness, temperance: against such there is no law. And they that are Christ's have crucified the flesh with the affections and lusts" (Galatians 5:22–24).

PART TWO

WHO IS THE GROOM?

And I beheld, and, lo, in the midst of the throne and of the four beasts, and in the midst of the elders, stood a Lamb as it had been slain, having seven horns and seven eyes, which are the seven Spirits of God sent forth into all the earth.
—Revelation 5:6

Who Is the Groom? Jesus Christ, The Head of the Church

Think not that I am come to destroy the law, or the
prophets: I am not come to destroy, but to fulfill.
—Matthew 5:17

The Holy Spirit shows me who God is. It was not that I did not know who God is, but I needed to be reminded who He is and needed to learn more about Him. Here is a small list of the big list the Bible has on who God is, how He is known, and what his plans are for us, his bride, his church.

Graphic 3: The Groom, JESUS CHRIST

GOD the Trinity	God
God the Father, God the Son Jesus Christ, God the Holy Spirit Colossians 2:9, 2 Corinthians 13:14, Isaiah 9:6	That exists by itself, Infinite, Eternal, Supreme, Incomprehensible, Sovereign, Transcendent-Without limit, The One God, Majestic, Omnipresent, All-Knowing, All-Powerful, Does Not Change-Is The Same Always, He is Spirit Isaiah 44:6
God Genesis 1:1	Jehovah Genesis 2:4
Holy Spirit John 14:26, 16:7, 13	I am who I am Exodus 3:14
Lord Exodus 34:23	God is love 1 John 4:7–8
The Lord, your provider Genesis 22:14	The Lord, your healer Exodus 15:26
The Lord who sanctifies Exodus 31:13	The Lord, your peace Judges 6:24
The Lord, your shepherd Psalm 23:1	The Lord, your righteousness Jeremiah 23:6
All-powerful God Genesis 17:1	Jesus Isaiah 9:6; Matthew 1:21, Luke 1:35

Some names Jesus is known by:	The Vine, Bread of Life, King of kings, my Rescue, the Messiah, Lion of Judah, Sheep, Warrior, Savior, our Lawyer, our Guide, Brother, True Life
Bread of Life, Teacher, Light of the World, Gate of the Sheep, the Good Shepherd, Life and Resurrection, the Way, the Truth, Rabbi, High Priest, Lord of lords, Friend	
"For I the Lord thy God will hold thy right hand, saying unto thee, Fear not; I will help thee" (Isaiah 41:13).	"Thus saith the Lord unto you, be not afraid nor dismayed by reason of this great multitude; for the battle is not yours, but God's" (2 Chronicles 20:15b). Read Psalm 97.
The Groom	**The Bride**
God paid the price for his bride, the death of his Son Jesus at the cross. Jesus was resurrected and has made a covenant with his bride, the body of Christ, the church, and one day he will return for her. He had to leave to go prepare a home, a mansion for us, his bride. Meantime He left us Himself, the Holy Spirit, to be with us forever.	The bride had accepted Christ as her Savior, so the covenant has been accepted and agreed on. While we wait, we need to keep living and believing and waiting upon Jesus Christ's return. The trumpet sound will announce one day the return of the groom who has come to rapture us his bride, the body of Christ, the church. One day we will have the wedding of the Lamb and celebrate!

Now to be that bride, you need to accept your groom, Jesus Christ, and pray diligently for you to be all his. Jesus already chose you, so now you have the choice to choose Him. Have you accepted to be the bride of Jesus? Have you accepted his marriage proposal? Are you anxiously expecting his return by being ready? Yes, I am ready, Jesus! Are you ready?

The Holy Spirit gives me more verses:

- "Furthermore then we beseech you, brethren, and exhort you by the Lord Jesus, that as ye have received of us how ye ought to walk and to please God, so ye would abound more and more. For ye know what commandments we gave you by the Lord Jesus. For this is the will of God, even your sanctification, that ye should abstain from fornication: That every one of you should know how to possess his vessel in sanctification and honour" (1 Thessalonians 4:1–4).

- "For Zion's sake will I not hold my peace, and for Jerusalem's sake I will not rest, until the righteousness thereof go forth as brightness, and the salvation thereof as a lamp that burneth. And the Gentiles shall see thy righteousness, and all kings thy glory: and thou shalt be called by a new name, which the mouth of the Lord shall name. Thou shalt also be a crown of glory in the hand of the Lord, and a royal diadem in the hand of thy God. Thou shalt no more be termed forsaken; neither shall thy land anymore be termed desolate: but thou shalt be called Hephzibah, and thy land Beulah: for the Lord delighteth in thee, and thy land shall be married. For as a young man marrieth a virgin, so shall thy sons marry thee: and as the bridegroom rejoiceth over the bride, so shall thy God rejoice over thee. I have set watchmen upon thy walls, O Jerusalem, which shall never hold their peace day nor night: ye that make mention of the Lord, keep not silence, And give him no rest, till he establish, and till he make Jerusalem a praise in the earth. The Lord hath sworn by His right hand, and by the arm of His strength, Surely, I will no more give thy corn to be meat for thine enemies; and the sons of the stranger shall not drink thy wine, for the which thou hast laboured: But they that have gathered it shall eat it, and praise the Lord; and they that have brought it together shall drink it in the courts of My Holiness. Go through, go through the gates; prepare ye the way of the people; cast up, cast up the highway; gather out the stones; lift up a standard for the people. Behold, the Lord hath proclaimed unto the end of the world, Say ye to the daughter of Zion, Behold, thy salvation cometh; behold, his reward is with him, and his work before him. And they shall call them, The holy people, The redeemed of the Lord: and thou shalt be called, Sought Out, A city not forsaken" (Isaiah 62).
- "Verily, verily, I say unto you, he that believeth on me, the works that I do shall he do also; and greater works than these shall he do; because I go unto my Father" (John 14:12).
- "Wherefore seeing we also are compassed about with so great a cloud of witnesses, let us lay aside every weight, and the sin which doth so easily beset us, and let us run with patience the race that

is set before us, Looking unto Jesus the author and finisher of our faith; who for the joy that was set before him endured the cross, despising the shame, and is set down at the right hand of the throne of God" (Hebrews 12:1–2).

- "All scripture is given by inspiration of God, and is profitable for doctrine, for reproof, for correction, for instruction in righteousness: That the man of God may be perfect, thoroughly furnished unto all good works" (2 Timothy 3:16–17).

- "And whosoever shall speak a word against the Son of man, it shall be forgiven him: but unto him that blasphemeth against the Holy Ghost it shall not be forgiven" (Luke 12:10).

- "Verily I say unto you, All sins shall be forgiven unto the sons of men, and blasphemies where with so ever they shall blaspheme: But he that shall blaspheme against the Holy Ghost hath never forgiveness, but is in danger of eternal damnation" (Mark 3:28–29).

- "Wherefore I say unto you, All manner of sin and blasphemy shall be forgiven unto men: but the blasphemy against the Holy Ghost shall not be forgiven unto men. And whosoever speaketh a word against the Son of Man, it shall be forgiven him: but whosoever speaketh against the Holy Ghost, it shall not be forgiven him, neither in this world, neither in the world to come" (Matthew 12:31–32).

- "If any man see his brother sin a sin which is not unto death, he shall ask, and he shall give him life for them that sin not unto death. There is a sin unto death: I do not say that he shall pray for it. All unrighteousness is sin: and there is a sin not unto death. We know that whosoever is born of God sinneth not; but he that is begotten of God keepeth himself, and that wicked one toucheth him not" (1 John 5:16–18).

- "If we confess our sins, he is faithful and just to forgive us our sins, and to cleanse us from all unrighteousness" (1 John 1:9).

- "For it is impossible for those who were once enlightened, and have tasted of the heavenly gift, and were made partakers of the Holy Ghost, And have tasted the good word of God, and the powers of the world to come, If they shall fall away, to renew them again unto repentance; seeing they crucify to themselves the Son of

God afresh, and put Him to an open shame. For the earth which drinketh in the rain that cometh oft upon it, and bringeth forth herbs meet for them by whom it is dressed, receiveth blessing from God: But that which beareth thorns and briers is rejected, and is nigh unto cursing; whose end is to be burned" (Hebrews 6:4–8).

- "There is therefore now no condemnation to them which are in Christ Jesus, who walk not after the flesh, but after the Spirit" (Romans 8:1).

- "No weapon that is formed against thee shall prosper; and every tongue that shall rise against thee in judgment thou shalt condemn. This is the heritage of the servants of the Lord, and their righteousness is of me, saith the Lord" (Isaiah 54:17).

- "For the law having a shadow of good things to come, and not the very image of the things, can never with those sacrifices which they offered year by year continually make the comers thereunto perfect. For then would they not have ceased to be offered? because that the worshippers once purged should have had no more conscience of sins. But in those sacrifices there is a remembrance again made of sins every year. For it is not possible that the blood of bulls and of goats should take away sins. Wherefore when he cometh into the world, he saith, Sacrifice and offering thou wouldest not, but a body hast thou prepared me: In burnt offerings and sacrifices for sin thou hast had no pleasure. Then said I, Lo, I come (in the volume of the book it is written of me,) to do Thy will, O God. Above when he said, sacrifice and offering and burnt offerings and offering for sin thou wouldest not, neither hadst pleasure therein; which are offered by the law; Then said he, Lo, I come to do thy will, O God. He taketh away the first, that he may establish the second. By the which will we are sanctified through the offering of the body of Jesus Christ once for all. And every Priest standeth daily ministering and offering oftentimes the same sacrifices, which can never take away sins: But this man, after he had offered one sacrifice for sins forever, sat down on the right hand of God; From henceforth expecting till his enemies be made his footstool. For by one offering He hath perfected for ever them that are sanctified. Whereof the Holy Ghost also is a witness to us: for after that he had said before, this is the covenant that I will make with them after those days, saith the Lord, I will put my laws into their hearts, and in their minds will I write them; And their sins and iniquities will I remember no more. Now where remission of these is, there is no more offering for sin. Having therefore, brethren, boldness to enter into the holiest by the blood of Jesus, by a new and living way, which he hath consecrated for us, through the veil, that is to say, his flesh; And having an High Priest over the house of God; Let us draw near with a true heart in full assurance of faith, having our hearts sprinkled from an evil conscience, and our bodies washed with pure water. Let us hold fast the profession of our faith without wavering; for He is faithful that promised; And let us consider one another to provoke unto love and to good works: Not forsaking the assembling of ourselves together, as the manner of some is; but exhorting one another: and so much the more, as ye see the day approaching. For if we sin willfully after that we have received the knowledge of the truth, there remaineth no more sacrifice for sins, but a certain fearful looking for of judgment and fiery indignation, which shall devour the adversaries. He that despised Moses' law died without mercy under two or three witnesses: Of how much sorer punishment, suppose ye, shall he be thought worthy, who hath trodden underfoot the Son of God, and hath counted the blood of the covenant, wherewith he was sanctified, an unholy thing, and hath done despite unto the Spirit of grace? For we know him that hath said, Vengeance belongeth unto me, I will recompense, saith the Lord. And again, The Lord shall judge his people. It is a fearful thing to fall into the hands of the living God. But call to remembrance the former days, in which, after ye were illuminated, ye endured a great fight of afflictions; Partly, whilst ye were made a gazing stock both by reproaches and afflictions; and partly, whilst ye became companions of them that were so used. For ye had compassion of me in my bonds, and took joyfully the spoiling of your goods, knowing in yourselves that ye have in heaven a better and an enduring substance. Cast not away therefore your confidence, which hath great recompense of reward. For ye have need of patience, that, after ye have done the will of God, ye might receive the promise. For yet a little while, and he that shall come will come, and will not tarry. Now the just shall live by faith: but if any man draw back, my soul shall have no pleasure in him. But we are not of them who draw back unto perdition; but of them that believe to the saving of the soul" (Hebrews 10:1–39).

- "Who shall separate us from the love of Christ? Shall tribulation, or distress, or persecution, or famine, or nakedness, or peril, or sword? As it is written, for Thy sake we are killed all the day long; we are accounted as sheep for the slaughter. Nay, in all these things we are more than conquerors through him that loved us. For I am persuaded, that neither death, nor life, nor angels, nor principalities, nor powers, nor things present, nor things to come, nor height, nor depth, nor any other creature, shall be able to separate us from the Love of God, which is in Christ Jesus our Lord" (Romans 8:35–39).

Purpose in Obedience!

As I write this, I believe and can say that I am complete! I am now sure of what I need to do with my life. This last time when I moved back to California, I remember hearing God telling me that I no longer would do the mission work in a physical way, meaning no more picking up and dropping off donations, physical labor. I was to continue doing the mission work but only in a spiritual way, but I did not really understand why and what exactly it meant. It was hard for me to not accept donations, especially because I knew they were needed and people who knew the ministry were willing to donate.

On so many occasions, my impulse and desires wanted to guide me to serve. I was tempted to do what I normally did, pick up and drop donations and then minister to those in need. Despite difficulty, I did not act on my impulse and desires, but I have been able to focus on doing God's will, to write and obey Him. Thank God for this time of fasting. I can now understand what it means to do spiritual mission work and no longer physical mission work. So, I will keep serving God, but the way He wants me to do it and not my way! With God, all things are possible!

This week's revelation will become a book that God gives me in memory of my time with Him. This is the spiritual mission work that God told me I would be doing! I am now a bride doing daily preparations for her wedding day! My purpose is revealed. Purpose in Obedience! Romans 8:28 comes to my mind, "And we know that all things work together for good to them (to whom? to Delilah), that love God, to them who are the called according to his purpose."

Thank GOD! Delilah trained by God to be used for bringing Revival! Restoring People's Lives!

I no longer have doubts; nor do I need any more confirmation from God. Now I believe, and I am going to obey and serve God!

In this fast, God gives me this book. I now laugh, and it is the laughter of joy. It took me a few years to know what God meant when He said, "Your book is complete." My 2014 vision is fulfilled today. This is found in chapter 1, image 3, the one called "The Vision." I am complete. I am healed and ready to share my life story through my book. I am not ashamed anymore and do not worry about what people may think or say about me when they find out what I have been through and what I have done. My books needed to be written in the right order, my life testimonies first. Then I can write other books, including a missionary book. How amazing! He is a God of order, fulfillment, and perfect timing! This makes me think of the Bible verse that says, and I am paraphrasing, we make our own plans, but then God comes and changes them. To God be the glory! I have a purpose in my life! He has changed my mourning into dancing! The Lord reminds me now of the two Bible verses he gave me at the beginning of this fast concerning where I was lacking in my spiritual walk, but no more! Now God is the builder of my home, and I have his knowledge. Thank you, JESUS!

- "Except the Lord build the house, they labour in vain that build it: except the Lord keep the city, the watchman waketh but in vain" (Psalm 127:1).
- "My people are destroyed for lack of knowledge: because thou hast rejected knowledge, I will also reject thee, that thou shalt be no priest to me: seeing thou hast forgotten the law of thy God, I will also forget thy children" (Hosea 4:6).

End of Seven-Day Fast: Thank You, Lord!

A week after this seven-day fast, the Lord would reveal more things to me that I had to add them to this book since all the teachings go along with what God had taught me. These teachings have added so much growth in my life and understanding, and I believe they are the main reason why I had to write this book. So, keep reading and discovering how wonderful and powerful God is.

Jesus Did It! So, I Can Do It Too!

Then saith Jesus unto him, get thee hence, Satan: for it is written, thou shalt worship the Lord thy God, and Him only shalt thou serve.
—Matthew 4:10

This study is based on Matthew 4:1–11, and here are the other verses used: Exodus 20:13; John 1:14; James 4:7; Revelation 1:8; Mathew 6:30–34, 27:35-37,59-60, 66,28:2,5-6 and Psalm 91:11-12.

The spirit of the Lord God was the one who took Jesus to the desert, and then the tempter, Satan, came with his sin, his lies. It is necessary to clarify this, so you do not get confused and think that God was the one who tempted. God does not tempt anyone because everything a person is tempted with is sin and God does not sin.

Physical Need: First Stone

Matthew 4:1–4

This passage tells us that the Spirit took Jesus into the wilderness to be tempted by Satan. Before this would happen, Jesus was baptized and had fasted for forty days. He was strong spiritually, but He was physically weak and hungry. Yet God allowed his Spirit to take Jesus into the wilderness right after the fast. While Jesus was there, Satan came to tempt him with food, the most urgent need of any human being, and Jesus was a human being. He had a physical body that needed food, clothing, rest, home, and love, but at that current time, the biggest need was food.

Let us see this verse, "And when the tempter came to Him, he said, If thou be the Son of God, command that these stones be made bread" (Matthew 4:3).

Satan is questioning whether Jesus is the Son of God and tries to put doubt in Jesus's mind about who Jesus is and wants to cause Him to disobey God. He asks Jesus to prove if He is the Son of God, to use his power to do a miracle by turning the stones into bread. The enemy offered to satisfy Jesus's hunger with something he found in the desert, rocks, and wanted Jesus to eat them so he could get sick and die.

Satan uses lies. He puts the word *if,* "if you are the Son of God." He never says what he knew to be truth, but he says what he believes to be his own lies. He used his weapon, lies and doubt, to attack and tempt Jesus. He thought that Jesus would accept because just like any human being, He was hungry and had to eat, but it did not happen!

Jesus could not ignore Satan's lies and accusations, but He had to answer him because He knew the Spirit brought Him there to be tested. Jesus is the Son of God, and He affirms his position and lineage and never loses control. We can see this with the answer given in Matthew 4:4, "But He answered and said, It is written, Man shall not live by bread alone, but by every word that proceedeth out of the mouth of God."

Jesus answered and defended himself, and He never submitted to sin or the enemy. He never doubted and therefore never disobeyed God because that is the result of doubt. If one falls, then you have disobeyed and sinned. It is important to notice the way Jesus begins his answer, "It is written." Yes, it is written. I can imagine that with this declaration, Jesus is saying, "There is nothing that you Satan can say or do to me because the Word of God is already written. Your end is already written! Yes, I triumph on the cross, and you lose the battle! I don't need bread to live but the Word of God, and I AM the WORD of GOD. I AM SELF-EXISTENT!"

We know that Jesus is God, the Word of God, the Verb that Became Flesh. So whatever way Satan attacks, he loses because JESUS IS THE WORD OF GOD. Jesus was tempted while being physically weak as a human being, but He did not fall into temptation. Jesus used his spiritual power to have victory in his physical and spiritual body. Jesus trusted God to provide his need for food and not the enemy! John 1:14 reads, "And the Word was made flesh, and dwelt among us, (and we beheld His glory, the glory as of the Only Begotten of the Father,) full of grace and truth."

Spiritual Need: Second Stone

Matthew 4:5–7

Jesus continues in this test, but now He is taken to another place. This time He is not taken by the Spirit of God, but by Satan, yes, and he takes Jesus to the Holy City and puts Him at the top of the temple. The enemy speaks to Jesus just like he did before; the only language he speaks is lies. Matthew 4:6 reads, "And saith unto Him, If thou be the Son of God, cast thyself down: for it is written, He shall give his angels charge concerning thee: and in their hands they shall bear thee up, lest at any time thou dash thy foot against a stone."

He says, "If you are the Son of God." We know what this means because we studied it in the first temptation, but let us review it again. He is questioning whether Jesus is the Son of God and tries to put doubt in Jesus's mind on who Jesus is and cause Him to disobey God. He asks Jesus to prove if He is the Son of God, to use his power to do a miracle to avoid death. This temptation escalated from the first one. Now it is no longer about food but is something spiritual and eternal, the soul. Now he is asking Jesus to renounce the authority of his Father God so He may be his own authority and decide when He dies. He is asking for Jesus to rebel against God.

This is the second time that the enemy uses the same phrase to try to put doubt in Jesus, but it does not work again! So, after he starts his sentence with doubt, then he tells Jesus to jump from this high building, the temple. He wanted Jesus to die but says, "You will not die because God will send his angels to save you." He told Jesus, "You will not die when you jump," meaning, "You are immortal." We know clearly that God is immortal, but Jesus had to be mortal as He came to be human just like us; therefore, He would experience death like all human beings.

To try to deceive Jesus, Satan uses Bible verses and attaches his lies. He could never say, "I made this" because he has never created anything in this world except for his lies. The correct Bible verse is Psalm 91:11–12, "For He shall give his angels charge over thee, to keep thee in all thy ways. They shall bear thee up in their hands, lest thou dash thy foot against a stone."

It would not be a small stumbling block that Jesus would have experienced if He had jumped from the high place of the temple. No, it would have been a death for sure due to the height, and supposing He was not dead but badly hurt, then Satan would try to finish his plot, to kill Jesus. Jesus would never entertain Satan's game and ask God to send his angels to save Him. Remember, God cannot be tempted, so Jesus jumping was never an option. This Bible verse says "ways." Is talking about wherever you may be going, and it does not mean what Satan said to cast yourself down, meaning throw yourself, jump, and try to kill yourself. No place in the Bible does it say that a person could take their own life. Only God can take our life and determine the day of death for each one of us. Exodus 20:13 says, "Thou shalt not kill."

Satan was tempting Jesus with death. He wanted Jesus to commit suicide. Oh, but he says, "You will not die!" He hides his evil plan behind God's Word, using it for evil, saying, "He will send his angels to carry you, so you don't fall against a stone." What? The enemy used a stone in his first temptation and once more again! The first stone, he wanted to put inside Jesus's body, and the second stone, he wanted to use it to hit the external body of Jesus. At the end, both plans were the same, seeking Jesus's death!

The enemy of God was tempting Jesus to die through suicide! He had chosen the date and time! Yes, Satan wanted Jesus to kill himself, and he picked the place to do it, the House of God, the temple! It could not be more humiliating! He wanted to humiliate Jesus in his own home! What would you do if someone comes to your own house to insult you and insist you kill yourself? Now you can see what is happening here.

But let us continue with these verses and see what Jesus did. Matthew 4:7 says, "Jesus said unto him, It is written again, Thou shalt not tempt the Lord thy God." Jesus would answer the same words that He said before and would add more words to correct the enemy, to let him know who is in charge! So, I can imagine that Jesus is saying, "What I told you the first time you tempted me, I repeat it again. It is written!"

Yes, Jesus says again, "The Word of God is already written, and I know my end and yours! I have the victory, and you lose! Yes, I triumph on the cross, and you lose the battle!" Let us see what else He said to the enemy, "Thou shalt not tempt the Lord thy God."

With this verse, I understand that Jesus is telling Satan, "I AM your GOD, though you do not accept it! I made you. I formed you, even if you don't want to accept it! So, I AM your GOD and have AUTHORITY over you, Satan, even though you don't want to accept it! I AM GOD-ELOHIM! You cannot tempt me, and you must not try! I never fall into any temptation! I AM WHO I AM! THE GREAT I Am, THE ALPHA AND OMEGA! I AM THE BEGINNING AND THE END!"

Jesus began the answer with authority and ends with authority, always making present WHO HE IS, HIS POWER AND HIS LINEAGE!

We know that Satan tried to prevent Jesus's birth, but he could not do it! He wanted to kill Him as a baby, but he could not do it! He wanted to kill Him as an adult, but he could not do it! It was GOD who would determine the day and time that Jesus would die. The death of Jesus would not be by suicide but by death at the cross for all of humanity's sins. His death on a cross, crucified by men and not of his own hands. Despite all his sufferings, he endured it all. Jesus fulfilled God's purpose and plans for his life.

Jesus trusted God for the day he would have to die, and that day came. JESUS became JESUS THE CHRIST! The glory belongs to GOD and only GOD! Mathew 27:35–37 says, "And they crucified Him, and parted his garments, casting lots: that it might be fulfilled which was spoken by the prophet, they parted my garments among them, and upon my vesture did they cast lots. And sitting down they watched Him there; And set up over his head his accusation written, THIS IS JESUS THE KING OF THE JEWS."

Emotional Need: Third Stone

Matthew 4:8–11

For the second time, Satan would take Jesus to a place to tempt Him, this time on a very high mountain. Matthew 4:8–9 reads, "Again, the devil taketh Him up into an exceeding high mountain, and sheweth Him all the kingdoms of the world, and the glory of them; And saith unto Him, all these things will I give thee, if thou wilt fall down and worship me."

Now Jesus was offered to have all He could see kingdoms, riches, and all its possessions of land, territory, money, things, and people. The tactic that Satan used was the last one he had left in his pocket. He put everything on the table, as we would say. Here comes the stone again. For the third time, he uses stones to tempt Jesus. This time he is using the stones to stand on and seeks to be worshipped there. He is using a mountain, and mountains are made of stones, rocks, dirt, and grass. He tells Jesus, "I will give you all this if you fall on your knees and worship me."

He is asking Jesus to kneel on the ground and submit to him. He is asking Jesus to depend on him for his emotional needs and to worship him as his god, and in return he can give Him power through the kingdoms and possessions. The emotional needs are love and affection, not possessions, but Satan does not possess love. Nor can he give love or affection.

Now let us see what Jesus did. Matthew 4:10 says, "Then saith Jesus unto him, get thee hence, Satan: for it is written, thou shalt worship the Lord thy God, and Him only shalt thou serve." Jesus puts an end to Satan and his temptations! Jesus would answer the same words like before and adds more words to correct him and to order him to leave. Jesus is the authority, and he lets Satan know by ordering him to leave his presence. I feel like this is how Jesus said it, "Oh, but before you leave, this is what you need to know," and Jesus repeats his same words and says, "What I told you the first time and second time when you tried to tempt me, I repeat it again for the third time: it is written!"

Yes, Jesus says again, "The Word of God is already written, and I know my end and your end. I have the victory, and you lose! Yes, I triumph on the cross, and you lose the battle! Jesus says you are to worship me only! You shall serve me only!"

And here we go again. ""I AM your GOD, though you do not accept it! I made you. I formed you, even if you don't want to accept it! So, I AM your GOD and have AUTHORITY over you, Satan, even though you don't want to accept it! I AM GOD-ELOHIM! You cannot tempt me, and you must not try! I never fall into any temptation! I AM WHO I AM! THE GREAT I Am, THE ALPHA AND OMEGA! I AM THE BEGINNING AND THE END!"

Jesus began the answer with authority and ends with authority, always making present WHO HE IS, HIS POWER AND HIS LINEAGE! Jesus only submitted and worship GOD his FATHER, Who is Love and All-Powerful.

Jesus applied the Word of God in his life. Remember He is the living Word, so He did what this verse says. James 4:7 says, "Submit yourselves therefore to God. Resist the devil, and he will flee from you." Jesus never accepted the stones that Satan was offering Him to satisfy his physical, spiritual, and emotional needs. In these three temptations, the enemy was asking the same, for Jesus to renounce being the SON of GOD and His Purpose in Life. We know that Jesus never fell into temptation, but He always exercised self-control. He ended the test when and how He wanted, depending on his Father God. This verse culminates with the end of Satan and Jesus's victory. IT IS WRITTEN! Matthew 4:11 says, "Then the devil leaveth Him, and, behold, angels came and ministered unto Him."

Jesus ordered the enemy to leave his presence, and he did! He had to submit to God and leave defeated! Once Jesus's enemy was gone, meaning the test was over then, God sent his angels to feed His Son Jesus. Jesus only accepted food from his Father! Jesus only lived the plans and purpose that his Father had for Him! Jesus only worshiped and loved his Father! Jesus only obeyed and submitted to his Father! Though weak, He endured all because He is the Son of God, and He proved it. But also, He endured all as a human being so we could have his testimony and see that JESUS DID IT! We have a VICTORIOUS JESUS! JESUS Is GOD, Who Is LORD Over All The Creation! Revelation 1:8 reads, "I AM alpha and omega, the beginning and the ending, saith the Lord, which is, and which was, and which is to come, the ALMIGHTY."

The Last Stone

A big stone was put in Jesus's tomb by his disciple, Joseph. He put a big stone on the tomb as it was customary when someone was buried for burial purposes as well as for protecting the body from animals and people and showing respect and love. Mathew 27:59–60 reads, "And when Joseph had taken the body, he wrapped it in a clean linen cloth, And laid it in his own new tomb, which he had hewn out in the rock: and he rolled a great stone to the door of the sepulchre, and departed."

A stone that was put out of love was then stolen by Satan as he was trying to use it as his last stone against Jesus. This time he wasn't trying to use it to kill Jesus because He was already dead, but it was to try to stop his resurrection. How did he think he could do that? Let us read Mathew 27:66, "So they went, and made the sepulchre sure, sealing the stone, and setting a watch."

The enemy believed that he could stop Jesus's resurrection and escape by having the tomb sealed and guarded. Since Satan could not kill Jesus, then he had to focus on destroying his reputation, thinking that God would be mocked when Jesus could not escape from the sealed tomb with the stone. He thought he could stop God's prophecy of being fulfilled, but he could not do it! Jesus won over death and transcended stones, walls, and spaces.

On the third day, Jesus appeared to people giving testimony of his resurrection. He fulfilled the prophecy! The Bible tells us that the tomb was empty before the angel of God moved the stone. JESUS Resurrects without having to move a stone and a guard! No stone and no one could stop JESUS from becoming the Savior of this World, of becoming JESUS CHRIST! Matthew 28:2,5–6 reads,

> And, behold, there was a great earthquake: for the angel of the Lord descended from heaven, and came and rolled back the stone from the door, and sat upon it…And the angel answered and said unto the women, Fear not ye: for I know that ye seek Jesus, which was crucified. He is not here: for he is risen, as he said. Come, see the place where the Lord lay.

Jesus Did It! So, I Can Do It Too!

Then saith Jesus unto him, get thee hence, Satan: for it is written, thou
shalt worship the Lord thy God, and Him only shalt thou serve.
—Matthew 4:10

Delilah P.I.O.

At the beginning of this book, you read my story on how God found me, how I was without hope, depressed, and being surrounded by death. Due to the painful stage I was in, I was easily tempted to give up on life because of my spiritual blindness. I could not see what was happening to me. I was defenseless because I struggled on having my faith and eyes on God, but my eyes were on my problems, my husband, and myself. And so, it did not allow me to see the enemy of my soul. Because of that, I did not have a plan of attack against the enemy or a way out! Thank God that He came to my rescue while depressed and while tempted with death. The Lord rescued me by telling me what to do and why, and I just had to obey Him to be delivered from death.

God's voice and instructions were so clear that I needed to fast for seven days because these demons only come out with fasting and prayer. Thank God for his revelation! My obedience to God, the fasting, and prayer brought me liberty from demonic attacks, liberty from sin and strongholds, and a new life! Thank you, Lord!

God has taken the veil off my eyes. I was deceived thinking that as a Christian I could not have strongholds or demonic attacks and that this only happened to a non-believer, a person who never accepted Christ as their Savior. This lie kept me prisoner because I could recognize that I needed to change the way I behave and think and that I was struggling with various sins in my life, but I didn't understand how this could be possible if I was a Christian. So, I was internally struggling to change, but I could not, and this kept me with lots of guilt.

What else could I do to change? I was doing what the Bible says. I would repent, pray, and walk away from sin but would fail again despite how much I desired to change. I would feel that I couldn't share my battles with anyone due to my fear of being criticized. How could I be struggling so much with these things if I had been a Christian and missionary for so many years? I was living like a religious woman without realizing it! I seemed to have it all together spiritually on the outside, but internally I was having too many internal battles. I could not realize what I lacked in character so I could be emotionally mature, accepting responsibility for my own actions and stopping the blame on others.

When Jesus died on the cross, He forgave all our sins, so the day I accepted Him as Savior, I was freed from all sins and strongholds. But as we walk our daily life, we can still have strongholds. That was the part I did not fully understand, and when I sought help for understanding, that leader could not help me. I am so thankful that the Lord kept teaching me, and now I clearly understand what a stronghold (chain) is and how it could enter a life. I didn't know that when I disobeyed God is when I brought strongholds to my life, and there were so many ways that I was being disobedient to God. I couldn't see that I was living in unforgiveness, with bitterness, rebelliousness, and much more. These strongholds had even caused sickness in my life, like my suffering of severe colitis and anxiety, but thank God, He delivered me! So now I know the difference and are no longer tormented with this sickness and the anxiety that comes with it. Praise God for this understanding and for delivering me after more than twenty years of sickness!

When it comes to the trials in my life, enemy attacks and temptations are just things that we must face as human beings since the fall of Adam and Eve. My reaction to my life challenges and situations were normal because as any human being, I could not avoid being sad, hurt, discouraged, and crying because I was going through so many problems in my life. I had to learn how to react to life situations now and not allow it to bring me down but obey God and trust Him with my life and its challenges.

Through my obedience to God, I can live free of strongholds and in the place that God has given me, assigned me to be, his Daughter, his Servant, being a head and not a tail. I learned that I need to live dependent on the Holy Spirit. To learn to know if it is Satan attacking me or if I am responsible for what is going wrong in my life. When the enemy brings a temptation to my life to be able to overcome it, I need to submit to God and use the Word, just like Jesus did, and this is how I resist the enemy so he can flee from me. To know if my thoughts and actions are right with God, I must ask myself these questions: are my thoughts, arguments, or things in my life against God?

If I answer yes to any of these questions, I must quickly rebuke. This means rejecting them from my life and asking the Holy Spirit guidance to help me live according to the Lord's will. Only the Bible, God's Word, can show us his will and what is against his will. So, I must filter through God everything in my life, putting everything under his eyes. I need God's discernment so I can distinguish the difference between my responsibility or when there are things that I do not have control over, like an enemy attack.

The examples I am giving you are what I have done in my life but thank God for his grace and for changing me. For example, if I get sick because I have been working so much and haven't taken care of myself and rested, I should not blame Satan, stating that he attacked me with sickness because I was the one who was responsible for it due to my lack of care for myself. If I insist on believing that I am not responsible, then I would be biblically wrong and would be making myself a religious and irresponsible person. In a case like this, I need to recognize that God has already given me health, so I need to be responsible to care for myself. It is not the responsibility of my husband, so I cannot blame him for it. And if I do not know how to care for myself, then I can ask God to teach me and help me stay committed to caring for my health. I do know that we can get sick sometimes, and that is not because of sin. But just because we are humans and our body can be exposed to so many viruses in this world, sometimes we cannot avoid but getting sick. God has helped me be aware of which foods to try to avoid so I will not have sickness in my mind, colon, and skin.

For example, if I am thinking that I am not worthy and nobody loves me, these are my imaginations. They are against God because if I were to read the Bible, I would find that God loves me. So, I must rebuke, reject these lies, obey God, and believe what his Word says, that he loves me and that I am his daughter, I belong to Him, and I am of worth. It is necessary that I know when I am under attack, and I need to remember that I am more than victorious through JESUS CHRIST! JESUS already Won and Defeated death on the Cross! So, this Victory is not optional for me because it is God-given, I did nothing to deserve it, but God gave it to me the day that I accepted him as my Lord and Savior. This is the same for you and everyone who accepts Jesus as Lord and Savior. You have been given Victory! Suicide is no longer a temptation for me because God delivered me and made me understand through the Bible and his revelations the true meaning of suicide and death.

Jesus was tempted, but He did not fall. The same power that is in Jesus is the same power that is in me. It is in every person who has Jesus as their

Lord and Savior. Death has no power over Jesus Christ! So, death has no power over me, but only Jesus Christ has power over us as believers!

Well, now I must be careful with my diet. I need to take care of what I eat and not make food an idol. The honey I ate during my fast was so sweet on my lips, and so it needs to be the Word of God in my life, but for this to be possible, I need to eat it and digest it so I can taste and enjoy it. This means that I must read, meditate, memorize, use it in my prayers, and believe it so I can walk with a sweet taste in my life. Taste and see that God is good. I must never accept the stones that Satan offers, pretending to satisfy my needs! I must always submit to God so he can supply and satisfy the following:

- Physical need: to eat food
- Spiritual need: to read the Word of God
- Spiritual need: salvation, purpose and eternal life
- Emotional need: to receive and give love and affection

Being tempted is not a sin but falling into temptation is a sin. I can overcome these three temptations when they come my way by submitting to God and believing that the blood of Jesus Christ covers me. I live with a purpose! And I will die the day that God determines, not the enemy! I can live like Jesus did. I only worship my GOD, and I only bow to my CHRIST. The enemy I had in the past; I will no longer see! Jesus did it! So did I! I am no longer a slave, but I am free, free of the chains of death! Hallelujah!

The Lord gives me this Bible verse. This is for me to always remember who my enemy is.

- "Ye are of your father the devil, and the lusts of your father ye will do. He was a murderer from the beginning, and abode not in the truth, because there is no truth in him. When he speaketh a lie, he speaketh of his own: for he is a liar, and the father of it" (John 8:44).

Then the Lord gives me these verses, so I always remember what his Word says to me, his daughter, and to us, his children.

- "Submit yourselves therefore to God. Resist the devil, and he will flee from you" (James 4:7).

- "But I will forewarn you whom ye shall fear: Fear Him, which after he hath killed hath power to cast into hell; yea, I say unto you, fear Him" (Luke 12:5).
- "Blessed is the man that endureth temptation: for when he is tried, he shall receive the crown of life, which the Lord hath promised to them that love Him. Let no man say when he is tempted, I am tempted of God: for God cannot be tempted with evil, neither tempteth He any man: But every man is tempted, when he is drawn away of his own lust, and enticed. Then when lust hath conceived, it bringeth forth sin: and sin, when it is finished, bringeth forth death. Do not err, my beloved brethren" (James 1:12–16).
- "So also Christ glorified not himself to be made an High Priest; but He that said unto Him, thou art my Son, today have I begotten Thee. As he saith also in another place, thou art a Priest for ever after the order of Melchisedec. Who in the days of his flesh, when He had offered up prayers and supplications with strong crying and tears unto Him that was able to save Him from death, and was heard in that He feared; Though He were a Son, yet learned He obedience by the things which He suffered; And being made perfect, He became the Author of Eternal Salvation unto all them that obey Him; called of God an High Priest after the order of Melchisedec" (Hebrews 5:5–10).
- "Seeing then that we have a Great High Priest, that is passed into the heavens, Jesus the Son of God, let us hold fast our profession. For we have not an high priest which cannot be touched with the feeling of our infirmities; but was in all points tempted like as we are, yet without sin. Let us therefore come boldly unto the throne of grace, that we may obtain mercy, and find grace to help in time of need" (Hebrews 4:14–16).

I was doing my Bible study on Moses and the Israelites, which I have read so many times but never like this before. After reading it, the Holy Spirit brought to my mind this scene. I felt like I could just see how the battle went on instead of me just reading words. It was an amazing experience and an eye-opener.

Graphic 4: Our Position during the Battle

And the Egyptians shall know that I AM the LORD, when I have gotten me honor upon Pharaoh, upon his chariots, and upon his horsemen. (Exodus 14:18)

Departure of the children of Israel from Egypt and the battle position: Exodus 12:41, 13:3–5, 17–22, 14:1–31

1 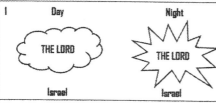		**First phase:** All of Israel leaves Egypt and marches free, with no yoke and no more oppression from their enemies. They know that day and night the Lord goes in front of them in a pillar of cloud guiding and a pillar of fire lighting the way, so they follow with peace. The Lord, the Angel of God, and Jehovah are all the same person, the Lord God.
2 Time of rest/Fear enters Jehovah says to Moses it's time to act, not time to pray! Moses uses the rod with power.		**Second phase:** Israel is at rest, but when they see the enemy following them, they have doubt and give into fear and ask for prayer. Jehovah tells them it's not time to pray but to act! He tells the leader Moses to lift his rod and use the power he has been given and to march with the Israelites!
3 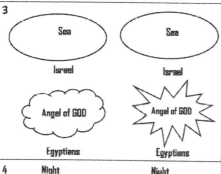		**Third phase:** Jehovah tells Israel what to do so he can destroy the enemy, and he then changes his position, the cloud and fire, to protect Israel and bring victory. Israel marches toward the sea; they needed only to stay in the assigned position and obediently walk no matter the time of the day. The enemy persecutes Israel from far away because they cannot get closer without getting hurt and dying! So there is a big distance between Israel and their enemies, and the Angel of God is in the middle, protecting them! Jehovah, the Lord, is using the cloud and fire as a protective and defensive position now!
4 Night Night Moses lifts his rod over the sea; Jehovah divides the sea 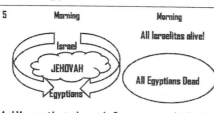		**Fourth phase:** Moses extends his rod over the sea, Jehovah divides the sea, and the impossible happens a miracle. A way out! Despite it being nighttime, Israel must go and not look at the time, so they go in the dry sea and walk in their miracle! They have to walk without having to pay attention to their surroundings. The Egyptians do not stop persecuting Israel, and they try to use Israel's miracle to destroy them! Yes, the enemy follows Israel into the dry sea with the intention of killing them!
5 Morning Morning All Israelites alive! All Egyptians Dead And Moses said unto the people, Fear ye not, stand still, and see the salvation of the Lord, which He will shew to you today: for the Egyptians whom ye have seen today, ye shall see them again no more forever. (Exodus 14:13)		**Fifth phase:** Jehovah tells Moses, "Extend your rod." The water returns to the sea, killing the Egyptians! Jehovah destroys the enemy who is in his territory—his miracle! God destroys the enemy in the morning so Israel can see it and they won't think that someone else destroyed them in the darkness. God is glorified! All Egyptians are dead! Israel is the only one who walked out of the sea alive! They had to just walk in the position God gave them with obedience and faith without intervening with God's battle plan! At no time did they have to put a hand to fight; they just witnessed Jehovah destroying the enemy! The enemy of Jehovah and Israel is destroyed! Victorious Jehovah! Victorious Israel!

My Application on How to Fight My Battles

And I, behold, I will harden the hearts of the Egyptians, and they
shall follow them: and I will get me honour upon Pharaoh, and upon
all his host, upon his chariots, and upon his horsemen. And the
Egyptians shall know that I AM the LORD, when I have gotten me
honour upon Pharaoh, upon his chariots, and upon his horsemen.
—Exodus 14:17-18

I thank God that He used this graphic to teach me all about the
battlefield and its positions. Having this knowledge has changed my life
so much, has given me that dependency on God that I needed to have, and
helps me be at peace. These are the five phases in the battle.

Phase One: Deliverance

Right after the Lord delivered me from my enemies, He shows me the
way to go. He walks in the lead position, showing me the way to fulfill
my calling and purpose in life. I obey by following Him. I walk right
behind Him as a new person that I am now free from all sins and chains.
I walk, believing in my salvation and God's promises for my family and
me. Walking like a head and not a tail! I am no longer a slave, but now I
walk believing and living in my freedom!

Phase Two: Time of Rest

When the time of rest comes, I need to obey. It is time for rest and to
do nothing else but rest! It is particularly important that I rest because if I
failed to do so, I would be weak for when the enemy attacks. So therefore,
I need to follow God's direction because He knows what is ahead for me.
I will obey and rest! I will eat, sleep, rest, and enjoy! When my time of rest
is over, since the enemy is quickly approaching, I don't need to give into
fear, despair, or worry or flee. Nor should I ask people what I should do or
pray, asking God, "What do I do?" God had already told me what to do,

to use the power He has given me. So, I must get up from my rest and go the way He showed me in the position He has given me.

Phase Three: Change of Position

Now I must walk in the lead position but not to forget that the Lord is right behind me, protecting me. He is in the middle between the enemy and me, for He is my protector and defender from my enemies and is going to destroy them all. I cannot stop or quit my walk. Also, I should not be wondering or asking myself, "Is God fighting for me?" or "What is God doing?" No, I should not be asking these questions because I should know that as soon as I see the enemy, God intervenes and destroys them. Only when I am in the right battle position can I walk with my hands up, praising and worshipping God.

Phase Four: Obstacles

No matter what my circumstances are, I must walk with faith, obeying God and using the power He has given me to remove the obstacles that are on my way. Is his power that is going to do the miracle! My deliverance is my miracle and no one else's! I should never allow my enemies to walk in my miracle! The enemy tried that with Israel, and God did not allow it. Nor did Israel. Instead, they kept walking and believing God. And this is the same thing I need to do, to keep walking with faith and obedience to God. No enemy of mine will use my miracle to destroy my life. No! This way out is only for me!

Phase Five: Victory!

This last stage of the battle is where I use again my gift with power, this gift imparted by the Holy Spirit to close the sea back, put back the obstacle, and destroy all my enemies with it! I close my miracle door because it was only for me to use, and by doing so, I destroy my enemies and bring honor and glory to God! As his child, now I can walk the life He has for me, which would bring Him glory.

No one can do what I am supposed to do but myself. So, I have to work on remembering that my table only has space for me, the writer. And it is my place, job, and responsibility to write and make my words come alive through my books and the stage for when I am invited to speak. I am the only one who can describe what God shows me and what I see and feel and let my emotions come out with transparency and so vividly so I could connect with people as I connect with God. My calling and job are never more important than God than my first ministry, which is my marriage and home, than my family and people. I always need to remember that because I do not want to be destroyed by my calling and job but give them their right place in my life. If I do that, the enemy cannot destroy me with my miracle, which is my life of freedom in Christ, having a calling and purpose, but I can live being a happy, productive worker and servant of God. I will always have threats of the enemy in my life, just like anyone else, but it is up to me how I react when they come my way. Do I give into despair, or do I submit my battles to God? When the enemy of my soul tries to come against my faith by attacking my life and everything that I am and have, I have a choice. What is my choice? I give my battles to God and take my position! From the beginning and until the end of the march, God will always provide for all my needs so I can reach my calling, my purpose in life.

Once I reached the place of my calling, then God will provide not just for my necessities, but He will provide overflowing. At this place is where my blessings will come and not just my provisions. I can be at peace now knowing and understanding how I need to live my life in Jesus Christ, living with the power of the Holy Spirit. Who fights your battles, you or God?

My Song to God

Then sang Moses and the children of Israel this song unto
the Lord, and spake, saying, I will sing unto the Lord, for He
hath triumphed gloriously: the horse and his rider hath He
thrown into the sea. The Lord is my strength and song, and
He is become my salvation. He is my God, and I will prepare
Him an habitation; my father's God, and I will exalt Him.
—Exodus 15:1–2

The people of Israel have just been delivered by Jehovah the Lord from the hands of their enemies, the Egyptians. Now they are no longer slaves and living oppressed, but they are free and on their way to the Promised Land and a new life! Moses, their leader, sings a song to God right after they are delivered, and the people joined him because all glory belongs to JEHOVAH! The lyrics of Moses' song tell the story about who the Egyptians were, what happened to the Israelites. It tells who God is and who he will always be and speaks of his power. It speaks of the victory they just experienced by God's hands, freedom from slavery! "And Miriam the prophetess, the sister of Aaron, took a timbrel in her hand; and all the women went out after her with timbrels and with dances" (Exodus 15:20).

After Moses and the people of Israel are done with their praise song, Miriam starts a new song. She is Moses' sister, and she continues worshipping the Lord God with a song, just like her brother did. Her praise to Jehovah God is so contagious that the women of Israel joined her. Miriam praises God with what she had and what she knew, to play the timbrel. We don't see her going from person to person asking, "Hey, do you have a harp I could borrow? You know I want to praise Jehovah because he just delivered us from our enemies, but I don't have enough instruments, do you think I could borrow yours?"

And the story could have continued this way, maybe by Miriam being distracted from doing what Jehovah the Lord put in her heart, to praise him. But the story did not continue that way; nor did we see Miriam asking or inviting the ladies if they wanted to join her in worship and praise. I would imagine that each Israelite was amazed by what they just experienced that they all willingly praised and worshipped Jehovah. They did it with their voice and everything they had and a thankful heart. To worship and praise God was the least thing they could do after what they had just experienced, the miracle and victory in the battle!

We were not there to see the terror, fear, abuse, poverty, sorrows, and much more of what the Israelites had experienced while being slaves in Egypt. We do have the accounts of what the Bible tells us though, of all the sufferings and labor they endured. All the suffering had forced them to plead to be rescued by Jehovah God. Just imagine that.

How do you plead? Have you ever pleaded to God or someone for mercy? Why did you do that? You were not pleading because you were happy and full of joy! No, a person pleads because they cannot take it anymore! Let me say this again: A person pleads because they cannot take it anymore! You have probably been there, and I for sure have been there many times in my life. So, with that understanding, we can now see why they are praising and worshipping Jehovah with their songs. Would you not be doing the same thing if you were just delivered from slavery and death? And after just witnessing the death of your enemies right in your face? You would not be feeling sad that the oppressor and persecutor of your life, family, and country has just been destroyed!

No, you would be happy and relieved! So, they were relieved that the ones that were trying to destroy their spirit, life, finances, culture, country, and future no longer existed! So, if that were me, I would be rejoicing in the Lord, thanking and praising Him, and doing that the rest of my life! To be grateful for life! Agradecida por toda la vida! So that's why Moses and all the Israelites were praising JEHOVAH, THE LORD ALL-POWERFUL GOD.

We know that their story does not end here because as you read the Bible and see the present time, the Israelites still have enemies that they encounter until this day. The Lord God is still fighting for them. You and I still have enemies that we will encounter too. And the Lord God is still fighting battles for us! But this story is about this moment, what they did after being protected and delivered and not forgetting it. Yes, not to forget what JEHOVAH, THE LORD ALL-POWERFUL GOD, has done for them! For me not to forget what JEHOVAH, THE LORD ALL-POWERFUL GOD, has done for me! And for you not to forget what JEHOVAH, THE LORD ALL-POWERFUL GOD, has done for you.

Oh, I want you to know that I did not always live this way of praising and worshipping God. For many years of my adult life, I didn't understand why people would raise their hands while praise songs were playing. I would ask myself, "Why are they crying or raising their hands during worship at church or at a Christian concert?" I was grateful with God, and I knew that people were grateful too but did not understand why you needed to raise your hands during worship songs or prayer time. I remember that many times I would arrive late at church, and I would miss most of the worship songs, arriving as they say, "Mexican time." I never felt bad since I thought that the most important part of the service was the preaching, the Bible teaching. And I did not just arrive late, but oftentimes I would be distracted during worship time and get irritated by how people worship. I would make excuses of why I could not participate during worship time, convincing myself that I could not sing because my voice was too harsh or that I did not know the song in that language but in another language. I had always liked worship music, and that was my problem because I only saw it as music but never as worship and praise to God.

After I accepted Jesus Christ into my life, I started to pray that God would give me a voice to worship Him through singing. He granted my wish and allowed me to be in a church choir as a preteen and then in a youth choir as a teenager with whom I did my first mission trip. I lost the desire to connect with God and to worship him through music when I walked away from him. When I walked back to God and started to attend the church, I started singing the worship songs because I always liked them. I would sing just to sing though; it was as if my singing were done for religious reasons and not because I could connect with the songs or words, much less with God.

Maybe you can identify yourself with me and may have the desire to change too and become a praise and worshipper of God. I shared with you in chapter 1 how this change came in me on one of my lowest days and how I connected with God through worship. On that day, I learned to play a worship song and make it into a prayer and as my worship to God for the first time in my life.

Since that time, I have learned the importance of why God created music and how this is a powerful instrument of his, besides being a form of art and something pleasant to the ears. He had taught me that the worship and praise songs are written and dedicated to Him, so I need to sing them with that in mind, using them with power to pray, worship, and glorify his name, to know that the enemy of my soul hates when I put all my attention on the Lord and may try to stop me from doing so. But once I start to worship the Lord God, the enemy has to flee!

As a believer, I must intercede in prayers for all those who are called to serve in the ministry of music, worship, and praises. Lastly, He taught me how I needed to obey his commandment of setting apart the day of the Lord. That belongs to Him. Therefore, the whole church service is important. It requires my punctuality so I could be part of the service from beginning to end. For when I arrived at the church, I needed to be ready to put all my focus on God and give Him all my praise and worship and to join the other believers as God dwells among our praise and worship.

With this understanding, I can praise God through worship songs and have become appreciative of the powerful ministry of praise and worship. It is with gratitude that I praise and worship my King, my God who rules over me. I have seen how the enemy over and over tried to destroy my life, but God has delivered me from evil, where no harm or evil can come against me because I belong to God and He is my defender! Oh, how much I love you, Lord, and desire you! Thank you that you have never let go of me from your hands despite all my disobedience and sin. Instead, you have forgiven me and still accept me as your daughter. Praise the Lord that I can worship Him with my five senses, with a healthy body and mind. Miriam and the Israelites chose to worship God.

I make that same choice every day, and it's willingly that I do it. Miriam used what she had, and I use what I have: my voice, cell phone, speakers, my whole body, and the floor! Here I come with all my volume to praise and worship my Jesus Christ, my Messiah! How do you praise and worship the King, Jesus Christ? "To cast out all thine enemies from before thee, as the Lord hath spoken" (Deuteronomy 6:19).

God does not change. He is the same God who has delivered Moses and the Israelites from the Egyptians. He is the same God who keeps delivering the remnant of Israel day by day from their enemies. God is still Israel's deliverer, and He will do whatever He needs to do in their lives, my life, and his people's lives so we can rest safe in his hands and focus on praising and worshiping Him. No enemy is bigger than our God! No one defeated death but Jesus Christ, and no one can defeat God! So let us remember that and keep praising and worshipping our KING, LORD, SAVIOR, DEFENDER, JEHOVAH-NISSI THE LORD OUR BANNER, GOD-ELOHIM WHO IS SOVEREIGN, RULER, AND OUR CREATOR.

Let us not spend time worrying but let us be at Jesus's feet and leave all worries there. Once there, then we can open our eyes to see who truly God is and how He has our life in the palm of his hands and who calls us the apple of his eyes. My battles belong to God, and I just need to focus on worshipping and praising Him!

Praise ye the LORD. Praise God in his sanctuary: praise Him in the firmament of his power. Praise Him for his mighty acts: praise Him according to his excellent greatness. Praise Him with the sound of the trumpet: praise Him with the psaltery and harp. Praise Him with the timbrel and dance: praise Him with stringed instruments and organs. Praise Him upon the loud cymbals: praise Him upon the high sounding cymbals. Let everything that hath breath praise the LORD. Praise ye the LORD. (Psalm 150)

Why Did You Move Me If I Was Better Off There?

And the children of Israel said unto them, Would to God we had died by the hand of the Lord in the land of Egypt, when we sat by the flesh pots, and when we did eat bread to the full; for ye have brought us forth into this wilderness, to kill this whole assembly with hunger.
—Exodus 16:3

When the Jewish people set out on their journey to the Promised Land, they needed food, but they complained and wrongly asked God for it. Not only did they ask to eat food, but they were asking for the food they were used to and which they already knew its taste. They did not think with a mind of explorers or travelers like, "Hey, let's see what kind of food we can look for and taste here in the desert." No, they set their minds and asked, "We want what we already know, what we like, and in the place where we're used to eating it!"

They were not willing to try new places and flavors and to get used to them. They had this negative attitude, thinking, "Why did you move me if I was better off there? God should have just killed us back home where we had food to eat." They quickly forgot carrying their yoke and their sufferings, so they were preferring to return to their known life. They did not remember the abuse and the long hours of forced labor. And what else? Living as slaves in poverty, crying, beatings, illness, death, and not being able to serve God. They did not remember how much they wept and implored God to help them, and for sure they did not recognize that leaving Egypt was part of the process of their answered prayer and that this new land, food, and places was what they needed to live now in their new life as free people and as they walk toward fulfilling their call, to live as the chosen ones and go to the Promised Land.

They did not remember the yoke that their enemies had upon them, that had over them but no more because God had already set them free! Oh, but they only think about their stomachs and what they lost: the loss of their daily snack, their lunch, their food, potato, or however you may want to call it! They did not see that the cost of that bite was too high price to pay. The cost was their lives, an awfully expensive bite! They could not see that God had made them free and that he was watching over them; therefore, He would provide food for them. But they were like Esau, the one in the Bible who sold his birthright for a bite. So, what were these Israelites trying to do after being freed? They were wanting to sell their birthright too! They were wanting to throw in the towel, and I say wanting because they did not since God did not allow it to happen, but instead they moved forward according to God's plans.

They had so many negative thoughts. Their thoughts of death blinded them to see and accept God's plans. Their lack of faith and vision could not allow them to believe that they could live a free and blessed life in the Promised Land. They were giving up because they thought that the only way for them to be guaranteed to eat food was by returning to Egypt and to keep living as slaves until the day of their death. Their thinking was that it would have been better to die by God's hands in Egypt with a belly with food and a full stomach than being free in the desert. The desert was not their Promised Land, but they could not see that or even think that far.

They had it clear that God gives life and that only He could take it away, but their actions did not demonstrate that. Instead, they showed that they did not really know God at all. They were not created just to be eating, and the food was not more important than them. Their life was about being and living free as God's chosen people. This freedom is something that goes beyond a meal for the day, a week, or a lifetime, but is about them living in the Promised Land and fulfilling God's plans and purpose for their lives.

How does God act in regards to the complaints and bad thoughts of the Israelites? God ignores their bad thoughts, complaints, and lack of vision and faith and gives them the food He has for them to continue their journey and reach the Promised Land. He had to ignore their complaints against Him and his leaders, Moses and Aaron, and their thoughts of slaves until death but with a full belly! Having a daily meal was what they wanted. How little they seek in their life. They for sure lack self-worth. These were not God's plans for their lives because they are his chosen people and bear his name. So, their option did not represent Him, and it was not what their leaders wanted for them, either because they knew God's plans for their lives.

The Lord God ignores their way of thinking and gives them food, unknown food. That is, they have the privilege of eating, and it is not just anything, even though they do not deserve it. But they eat food that no other human being had the privilege of eating here on earth. This shows us God's forgiveness, love, mercy, special care, and grace toward them.

I think that maybe a church leader might have given up on helping people like them and would have walked alone to the Promised Land. But Moses was not living in disobedience but obeying God as a leader, despite how hard it was. Moses represented God so he had to show self-control, wisdom, obedience, authority, humbleness, love, and a forgiving heart and to leave everything in God's hands. Moses and Aaron did not have the Israelites in their hands, but they left them in God's hands. That is how they were able to ignore their complaints and not take them personally because they knew their role, to be the leaders for God's chosen people. That is why these leaders were able to tell them God's message, "We'll eat tomorrow. We'll be blessed with the glory of God."

So that is why they were able to say, "Everything is forgotten, and let's enjoy this food and be ready to be before God tomorrow." The dignity was not on the Israelites but in who they represent for God and the world, and eternally. They are the remnant of ISRAEL. That is why they ate and saw the Glory of GOD! It was not because the Israelites deserved it, but because GOD-ELOHIM is their GOD, And It's Who They Represent. We have a God who loves us, forgives us, gives us his mercy and grace, and allows us to see his glory because WE ARE HIS PEOPLE, HIS CHURCH! Hallelujah!

I Cannot Give Up!

Two months had elapsed since I had my seven-day fast. I had reached out to the marriage pastor at our church a month after my separation in hopes that he could help us. At the same time, I reached out to a few male leaders of the church to get prayers to be accountable and in hopes that they would reach out to my husband. I didn't want him to be isolated from the church and man because of what we are going through, especially because we aren't communicating or seeing at all. I have not kept myself isolated. I am blessed by being surrounded by some of my godly friends, and I knew my husband needed that too. Any person going through things in life needs friends, no matter how embarrassed or hard what we are facing, our friends can help us through it and become the family that we so much need.

I counted on my friends when it was time to move out. For the move, it was only the two of us, my son and me, because I was still separated from my husband after more than two months. I previously decided to not rent a place since I could not afford it, especially in California. I had asked friends if we could stay with them in the meantime, and we did. I am truly blessed with great friends. I planned to remain in California, and once my son graduated and went to college, then I would move to Mexico if no reconciliation had happened in my marriage, even though I was waiting for God to do a miracle in my marriage.

I had to stop the phone communications with my husband since they were not good. They were just damaging the relationship more, and I did not want this to push me to give up on my marriage. I probably could have asked my husband to get together and just keep living like we always did, but I knew it was not good at all. I longed to see more of the caring and loving husband instead of the anger and other issues we were experiencing. It is only God who could bring it forth; only he could show him what he needed to do and not me, to know what his place and responsibility were as my husband.

My son had lived with us, and everything affected him too. I did not want that life for me or my son. I had failed in this my third marriage, and I had left that in God's hand. I was now focusing on what I needed to do, to be the best mother I could be for my son Moses.

My priorities were to make sure that we had a place to live and that I continued helping my son with his education and future. With God's help and strength, I spent months driving to places for us to stay. Sometimes we would spend three days in a home, and then we had to move again. Two homes were close by; another one was out of our city, and the other one was out of the country in Tijuana. For the one in Mexico, we could only stay on the weekends, when my son had no school activities, which was just a few times. When we couldn't stay in any of the homes, then we stayed in a hotel.

Before we moved from our home, I had assured my son that he did not have to worry about where we would live because that was my job. It was not an option to stay on the streets or in the car because God had already provided for us to have a place to stay. I would drive for more than four hours a day when we stayed far away so we had to wake up at 5:00 a.m. and make breakfast and lunch for my son while he would get ready. We always arrived on time at his school at 7:00 a.m. Thank God! Once I would drop off my son at school, then I would find a fast-food restaurant where I could drink a coffee and eat my breakfast or buy one for under three dollars.

Then I would spend time studying the Bible. praying and then writing. I did not allow the circumstances in my life to stop me from writing, but I continued, remembering that in due time I would do everything that God had called me to do. I had to learn how to work under pressure. Oh boy, what a pressure! I had to learn how to write at a well-known fast-food restaurant, to work with the TV on, people talking, noises and smells around me, and many distractions, but I was able to do it.

In my mind, I would say, "This table and chair where I am sitting is my private office at a large corporation." Only because of the process God had taken me through is how I could work with all those distractions; I had learned to be still and no longer struggle with having a preoccupied mind and body. I have been trained by God and for his service. This allowed me to work for months without a permanent home. During these whole months, I was just interrupted for a few times, but they were all divine appointments, either it was because I needed a break or encouragement or to encourage someone.

I am going to share one of my divine appointments. A friend from church whom I had not seen for a while came to this restaurant and said hi to me. She had no idea what I was going through, and I did not share it with her either. It was not the time. She thanked me for helping her son and family with the application for a school grant and other information on college. She was full of joy and with praise reports about how her son and their life had changed so much since that day, and she thanked me for helping them. I was overwhelmed with joy and could only express to her that I was just an instrument to God our provider, that it was a blessing to have helped him and to now hear their testimonies. All the glory to God! An absolute divine appointment! I was so happy to see her and hear her praise report. Once I was done with my writing, I would spend time on my son's needs and try to see how I could make life better for the two of us.

After using the restaurant bathroom for a while, I made the best decision I could make. I spent some money on a gym membership where I was able to use showers, the bathroom, and the treadmill for exercise to help me relax. Being able to do all this helped me feel like a normal person and not the feeling of being displaced, homeless. For lunches, I would eat my food or purchase food when necessary but avoid expensive meals since I needed to use the money to provide for my son. He needed things for school and his daily living, and because he was in sports, he needed healthy snack bars and drinks that were a little costly.

Every two months I needed to buy him running shoes, and now we were having his graduation expenses and other things. The dollars I had saved for when I was with my husband provided for me, and I used the child support money to provide for my son's needs. And on some occasions, I had to use my credit card for the hotel and graduation expenses and couldn't stress about it because I had to care for my child but just use my card carefully, which is what I normally did.

I did not grow up using credit cards, so since the day I received one in America, I have tried to not live by credit but to live within my means. Throughout my life, I have had to use my credit card and incur debt but always tried paying it off in time, and this was what I was going to do again. But for now, I must focus on providing for him even if it means that for few months, I might need to use my credit card, at least until I figured out about my job and place of living.

My car, besides being my way of transportation, became my place of prayer, crying, and rest and napping. Thank God for this vehicle. My sons never turned their backs on me; nor did they blame it on me for what we were going through in our lives, especially Moses, who was living it firsthand. He would get up every day and do what he had to do to focus on school and his track meets. He would have to help me every time we had to move, to pack suitcases, and then help me get them in and out of the car or place of stay.

Normally when my son had track meets, we did not arrive home until midnight since they finished late and because we were staying far away. I did not care because these meets kept him motivated, and I was happy to see my son run and do great in his competitions despite all the things that he had to endure.

When we lost our house, I had to put our biggest things in a storage facility and keep some in the trunk of my vehicle, and we only had what we needed with us. I could have moved my son to another school since my friend who lived far away offered us her home as long as necessary. I was thankful for her kindness, but I had to do what was best for my son and avoid having another change in his life. I had to drive many times tired and with a lot of pain in my left arm, always asking God to keep us well, and he did. I had movement in my left arm, but it was very painful for me, and then I lost the power to lift it so I had to rely on my son's help many times. At times we stayed in a house near the school, which would give us a break because we could sleep a little longer and spend less time in the vehicle.

A Dream of Liberation!

And it shall come to pass in the last days, saith God, I will
pour out of My Spirit upon all flesh: and your sons and
your daughters shall prophesy, and your young men shall
see visions, and your old men shall dream dreams.
—Acts 2:17

My husband and I started communicating again after three months of separation. He reached out to me via phone, and we set a day to meet again, but neither of us was ready. That short visit led us to just hurt each other and lose our patience. In my desperation, I gave up on my marriage and filed for divorce. I had filed twice for divorce in this marriage. The first time happened within the first year of marriage, but then I cancelled, and now I filed again. This second time when I filed, my husband disagreed, but he still signed it. God would not allow me to continue to live in disobedience, so He spoke to me through a dream on the day when I filed for divorce this second time.

That night I went to bed, and I had this dream that I was pregnant and in a small hospital room. I was giving birth to a nine-month-old baby, but I was six months pregnant. I was lying in bed and standing in front on my right side was my husband, but his face was a little hard to distinguish because it was very blurry. He was standing there, looking at me while I was giving birth. Clearly in my dream, I could see that standing in front of my left side was a man all dressed in white. There were just the three of us in the room. I was about to give birth, all natural.

The person dress in white did nothing to help me. He was quiet and only looked at me. After so much pain, I had a natural birth, and what came out was pure blood. I did not have a baby but a sack of blood! Neither the man in white nor my husband helped me. They were only standing as spectators, and that is how my dream ended.

Next day when I woke up, I remembered the dream. I got scared so I prayed. I asked God to reveal to me the meaning of this dream if he gave it. I did not understand it, and I wondered what it might mean. I thought, *I can't get pregnant anymore because I no longer have a uterus. So, I think this is what my dream means. I just filed the divorce, and in six months it ends. This dead marriage ends in six months, and all my suffering is going to end.*

This was not the meaning of this dream though. Thank God I began to have conviction for what I had dreamed and for my disobedience to him. Months before this dream, God had told me that I was never going to take divorce as a solution for my marriage problems. I was done doing that, but nevertheless, I had done it again! A few days after this dream, God revealed to me its meaning, that I was carrying death. That is why I did not have a baby but gave birth to blood only. In my body, since I was the one who was pregnant, I was carrying a pregnancy of death.

After this revelation, I felt fear and asked God for forgiveness. Never in my life had I known this, that divorce is death. I know that divorce carries destruction, but I had never seen it as death before until now. I was carrying that. I was carrying my third marriage to the same path, death! But it was over. No more!

I prayed, "Lord Jesus, I don't want to carry that. It was horrible in my dream, and it's been horrible in my life. Forgive me."

I thanked God for his revelation, and I continued to be focused on being obedient to Him, despite not having reconciliation in my marriage. I still had questions about one part of my dream. Why did the man and my husband did nothing to help me?

After a few days, I shared my dream with a Christian lady, who interpreted the rest of it. Thank God for her. She asked, "Do you know why they didn't help you? The person in white was Jesus Christ, and He could not help you bring death. Yes, Jesus could not help you get divorced, and that is why He was just observing. You were the one who was doing everything!"

God does not sin, and my divorce was a sin because I had no biblical foundation for divorce. I was so amazed at this great revelation from God. Then she said, "Your husband signed the document, but you were the one who filed, the one doing this all alone." That is why my husband's face was so faded. I excluded him and pushed him away from my life when I filed for divorce. I thanked her and God for the complete revelation of this dream. This revelation was what God would use for me to not give up on my marriage. I continued praying and believing in his promises.

I was just like the Israelites. I was trying to go back to my life of slavery. Thank God for this dream and that teaching, which helped me to not go back but to move forward and be in prayer and believing God's promises for my life. When discouragement or attacks came my way, I wore my armor, read the Bible, and then read pages of this book to remember what God had taught me and freed me from.

Keep Up the Fight!

I avoided having to interrupt my son's daily routine despite our circumstances, so I made sure that he continued in sports and spent time with his friends when possible. We both kept attending church as usual, during the week and on Sundays. No distance or trial would stop my son and me from being in the Word and with other believers. Due to all the circumstances, we were facing, at times my relationship with Moses was extremely hard because we both were too overwhelmed by what was happening in our lives and our personalities would clash too. I knew that I could not overcome my trials alone.

No matter how much I prayed and fasted, I needed my friends. So, to help me overcome my life problems, I would reach out to my few friends with whom I could talk, pray, and cry when I needed it. I knew that my son needed to share his burden and talk about it with someone, but I did not think he was getting to do that because as young people sometimes they keep it all to themselves. My son was carrying the burden of living with his separated mother and taking the role of being the only male at home and only helper. I knew it had to be hard to hold his feelings of frustration, anger, and much more and instead try to focus on his life as a young adult that he was becoming. At times I could tell that my son wanted to just run away because he was pushed too far away by me or our circumstances.

So, I sought for my son to have someone to talk with at church and school when he needed it. I wanted to make sure that he knew that help was there when needed and not just on the day when he had to meet with them for counseling. These were extremely hard times. He was in his last months of classes and having to focus on graduating and sports, and on top of that, he had to deal with having to move every few days every week. Also, he had upon his shoulder the responsibility that he was going to be living alone because he would be going to study and live at the university, which was in another city far away from me. So, I had to make sure that I helped him and focused on putting all my efforts and time, even if I was exhausted, because I could not fail him anymore.

One day I had an argument with my son, and we both exploded that I lost control and asked him to leave the house, and he did. On that night, we were staying in a home in our city, close to our church and his school. As my son left, I was able to reconsider and realize that our fight had not been because of what we had talked about, but that the problem was that we were both physically and emotionally exhausted. I cried a lot and felt that I could no longer carry my burden as a single mother, so it was best to go to church to get prayer and have someone to talk with. I was looking for someone to talk with my son, but this did not happen. Instead, some ladies prayed for my son and me. Then I stayed talking to one of them, who was my friend.

This friend said to me, "Satan wants something you have, Delilah."

I said, "Oh, I know what he wants. He wants my faith. He wants me to renounce it and to give up on my life and my children's lives, but I'm not going to do it!"

She then added, "Go home, sister. Go in peace because God is with you and your family."

I replied, "Yes, I will leave like that, with much encouragement and remembering all of what God has taught me!"

This friend had hosted us at her home, and she knew the difficulties we were facing. I went home, and when I arrived, I said to myself, "I cannot give up! My son needs me, and this is not the life God has for us or the relationship I should have with my son. I want my children to be happy and achieve their dreams. My children belong to God, and I will fight for them and God's plans for their lives!"

I then prayed for forgiveness from God for losing my patience and control with my son. I also prayed that my son would forgive me and not hold a grudge but return home. I also asked God for protection from enemy attacks on our lives and focused on all his plans for my precious children. I was able to sleep and rest that night in peace. I got to see the separation as a break for my son and me. He was able to stay at the home of a school friend, and in the meantime, I rested from so early mornings and driving. I spent time seeking God's direction on how best to help my son and what to do to have a better relationship with him.

One of my friends helped me better understand my son, and in response to this, I sent a letter to him on his cell phone. In this letter, I expressed how sorry I felt to have a broken marriage, to have hurt him, to fail him, and asked to forgive me. I expressed how bad I felt about not being able to offer him a permanent house, but that he could continue to count on me as usual. I wanted him to know how proud I was of him for who he is and for being well-focused on his goals that he was worthy of all my respect and much more. From now on, I would be treating him as an adult and no longer as a child, and I asked him to forgive me for not doing it sooner.

I told him how much I loved him, the gift and blessing he is for my life. This letter was longer than this, but basically this was my message, for him to forgive me and make him see my great love for him, remind him of God's love and plans for his life, and offer him all my support and ask him to allow God to heal him and our relationship. I could not repair all the brokenness in my son, but I could love him and give him all my support and allow God to heal him and our relationship.

My son answered me right away with a text with beautiful words and came back to live with me again. We were only separated for a few days, and we were able to continue to have a better relationship. I had never had such a problem with him and was so grateful to God and my son for having such a forgiving and loving heart.

During all this time of trials, Gershom, who was far away at his university, continued in communication with me and making sure that we were well. Sometimes when we spoke, he would ask me to be patient with my husband and give him time despite me not understanding him. I was amazed by my son's ability and heart to intercede for my husband and helping me understand my husband as a man and the things he was facing in life. This son offered to focus on finding me a place to live after his younger brother graduated. I knew he was also devastated by everything we were going through again, but he was trying to not show me, but he put his focus on seeing that we were well. I thanked him and was able to tell him what my plans were, but that I was waiting on God because I no longer wanted to take decisions lightly.

Moses graduated from high school despite all the difficulties he had to face. He finished well in sports too, participating in all the track meets and finishing all races with great success! On the week of his graduation, I spent that whole week with excitement and much crying because of what he had accomplished. I was so proud of him. All his hard work and sacrifices had paid off! As a mother, I felt relief too that I no longer needed to worry about him and of not having a place to live because soon he would be attending college and living at the dorms. I was grateful to God for helping my son graduate and giving me the strength to care for him so he could finish this school cycle well. To celebrate his graduation, we ate dinner and were joined by Gershom, Moses' father, and stepsiblings. We had some of my close friends at this celebration too, and together we all celebrated Moses and his achievements!

As for my health, I continued with much pain and lack of movement in my left arm, and oil massage and prayer were what would bring me some relief. I was convicted about holding things against my husband, so I repented and forgave. This would bring instantly some healing to my arm. Though I was still in pain, I had made up my mind that I would not allow this affliction on my body to stop me from moving on. I continued to focus on obeying and trusting my marriage to God and with the expectancy of miracles to happen in my life and my sons' lives.

God continued to use the life of David, the King, to make me see how I had something in common with him. For I love the Lord passionately and want to please him, to bring him glory just like David did. Like David, I had to accept that I am a fragile human being and a sinful one too. Finally, I could see what God saw in me! I, Delilah, never lost the call, to share the Word of God, and I will do so now through my books and speeches. Before I was the person I am today and before I became a bilingual writer, I had been a maid, sales agent, clerk, secretary, receptionist, administrator, business owner, graphic designer, teacher at a high school and children's ministry, missionary, leader, social worker and mentor.

I can see how all my job experiences have been for my good, to fulfill my purpose in life. God has used everything I have ever done in my life, even the bad and difficult things for my good. The good and bad experiences in my life made me the woman I am today. No bad decisions, sufferings, pains, poverty, homelessness, or trials as a mother and woman could stop me from being the woman that God made me to be and live the life, He has for me! I am a woman who is still standing strong with my faith in God, my family, and humanity. I am standing because of the power of the Holy Spirit in me, which gives me a passion for living an abundant life! I have a great family lineage and a great Christian lineage too, the one of Christ my Savior. I am a warrior and a very persistent one! All the battles and enemy attacks could not stop me from living my life abundantly and pursuing My GOD, My KING, and SAVIOR JESUS CHRIST! May my life continue to bring Glory to JESUS CHRIST! May my lineage continue to bring Glory to The LORD GOD ALL-POWERFUL!

What man is he that feareth the Lord? Him shall He teach in the way that he shall choose. His soul shall dwell at ease; and his seed shall inherit the earth. The secret of the

Lord is with them that fear Him; and He will shew them his covenant. Mine eyes are ever toward the Lord; for He shall pluck my feet out of the net. (Psalm 25:12–15)

I Am Loved!

For God is not unrighteous to forget your work and labour
of love, which ye have shewed toward his name, in that
ye have ministered to the saints, and do minister.
—Hebrews 6:10

It was with this phrase that I started my prologue, the phrase I had written in my diary, "No man can satisfy me until I am satisfied with My Great I AM—Jesus! If God has a missionary husband for me, He will provide it, and if not, I accept my singleness."

Marriage to God is more than those words I have written in my diary. Through the process, God has taken me. I now learned that it was not a title or job position that I needed for my husband-to-be, like how I wrote in my diary, a "missionary husband." But it was a husband I needed. This is a person, a man who could love me and complete me as a woman. God had to heal my brokenness and complete me so I could receive and give love.

In order to love my husband, I had to learn to go to the cross daily and be the bride of Jesus first since that is the only way I can be satisfied with My God, My Great I AM. And there is where I discovered that I am Loved! I am loved by God, and it is only there where He keeps filling me with his love. Then and only then is when I could love and accept my beloved, my husband. I must now focus on making decisions based on the counsel of the Holy Spirit and not on my emotions.

My husband contacted me after being without communication for a month, and by now we had already been separated for five months. We agreed to meet. I now felt ready and that it was the moment I had hoped for. This would be the day when God would give me the opportunity to show my obedience and love for him and my husband. I met with my husband during the day, and after we greeted each other, I was silent. I let him speak, and I heard everything he wanted to tell me. I had prayed earlier on that day that God would keep me quiet and that I would just be a listener. It would be my husband who would express on his own will what changes needed to happen in him and our marriage.

He spoke and then asked me for forgiveness, and I did the same. We forgave each other and decided to start over in our marriage. Finally, my miracle happened, the reconciliation in my marriage! I immediately canceled the divorce papers and gave my word to God, husband, and children that I would never file for divorce in my life again. Then we both spoke to my sons and asked for forgiveness, and they both forgave us.

While we were separated, my husband had started taking an anger and management class at our church and finished once we were back again. Also, we took a few months of Christian marriage counseling with a married couple from our church. Another good change in our marriage was that my husband accepted for me to become a writer and gave me his support.

I have been reminded that marriage is sacred to God and that He made it to be only between a man and woman. Each love relationship in my life has never satisfied me because none gave me what I needed and desperately wanted, which was true love. There is not a man, a human being, or thing created that could love me with that real love and completeness that I have searched for my whole life because only God could love me that way as only, He is love. He is the only one who can supply all my needs, and only He is who I want to depend on. To supply my need for the love of a man, God created the man and marriage, and we can find these in Ephesians 5:21–33 which says:

> Submitting yourselves one to another in the fear of God. Wives, submit yourselves unto your own husbands, as unto the Lord. For the husband is the head of the wife, even as Christ is the head of the church: and He is the saviour of the body. Therefore as the church is subject unto Christ, so let the wives be to their own husbands in everything. Husbands, love your wives, even as Christ also loved the church, and gave himself for it; That He might sanctify and cleanse it with the washing of water by the Word, That He might present it to himself a glorious church, not having spot, or wrinkle, or any such thing; but

that it should be holy and without blemish. So ought men to love their wives as their own bodies. He that loveth his wife loveth himself. For no man ever yet hated his own flesh; but nourisheth and cherisheth it, even as the Lord the church: For we are members of his body, of his flesh, and of his bones. For this cause shall a man leave his father and mother, and shall be joined unto his wife, and they two shall be one flesh. This is a great mystery: but I speak concerning Christ and the church. Nevertheless let every one of you in particular so love his wife even as himself; and the wife see that she reverence her husband.

I was so busy dealing with one more marriage failure that I had forgotten about the desires of my heart and purpose, but God did not. But instead, He used this, my last marital failure, to change my life, and only by surrendering to him, my husband, marriage, and everything about my life was how He could do it. God did not forget that I had accepted Him as my Savior and that I had prayed to surrender to Him and his will as a young teenager. The Lord God does not forget us or the plans He has for us, but with his amazing grace, He reaches us and shows us the way. By marrying, I interrupted the process in which God was taking me, which was to be completely his so I could live the life He has for me. This interruption was not caused by my marriage, but by me because I laid my eyes on my problems, my husband and me, which caused my depression and other problems.

I thank God that He did not leave me in the state I was in but rescued me from my carnality and the clutches of the enemy. Then He returned me to the place where I paused with Him and then took me step by step until I reached the final step. I could have never achieved by my own means, the restoration and transformation of my life as a daughter and disciple of God, woman, wife, and mother without having to go through this whole process of God. The final process is of experiencing revival in my life. I am blessed to live as a woman whose life has been restored and completed by the Holy Spirit. Thank God who showed me how much I am worth!

I returned into my marriage as the woman I am, a woman with a healthy and complete heart by God through his Son Jesus Christ and the

Holy Spirit. I returned, knowing now that I am loved by the Lord and that I love Him and so want to share that same love with my husband. I accept my husband's love and care for our home and me. I now know my limitations and those of my husband when it comes to giving and showing love and affection so I can't be disappointed in them but accept the fact that God made us that way and that He is the only one who can completely satisfy us, his creation. That is why He sent his Son Jesus to die on the cross so we could all have an opportunity to have his love and live eternally with Him.

God created marriage, family, friends and neighbors so I can give and receive love and affection. And now I know which type of love to expect from each one of those relationships and how to love them back, knowing the limitations that our human love has. No person, animal, place, or thing shall ever take God's place in my life, but I need to give each its rightful place, and by doing so, I will obey God and live with his peace and blessings. I am committed to God and my husband and put all my effort into my marriage. I am always working on my relationship with my husband and having the patience to know to wait on God when things are not going well. It is beautiful to be able to live, giving God his rightful place in my life as my God and King who rules over me. Also, to give my husband his God-given place in my life as the leader, provider, and protector of the home. He is my companion and the man who completes me as a woman and whom I love and respect.

As part of my restoration, God healed my physical body as well. I spent a total of fourteen months in much pain on my left arm and followed the doctor's advice. I scheduled surgery in hopes to fix my arm. I did not need to have the surgery because one day before the surgery I was healed. I had full movement and no more pain, God's miracle! Now I can move my arm and live painlessly, I can write, and I can raise my hands and praise and glorify God!

As for my sons, Moses got to study away from home at his dream university. I could think back on the day when my son told me that he was thinking of other options in case he could not go to college. This was because of the finances and everything else we were facing due to the marriage separation. To help him, I was able to encourage him to focus on one option, to focus on going to college and achieving his goals because no one else could do it for him. Also, while still separated, I took Moses to visit his dream university in San Francisco, and Gershom joined us for this trip.

We had a wonderful time just the three of us. I was privileged to have both of my sons pursuing an education and being focused on their dreams and that they allowed me to be part of it. The trip really helped Moses and made him stronger. He focused on attending college and continuing running in track. To make sure he was taken care of, I did my part as a mother and helped him apply for scholarships. Moses enrolled at Academy Arts University, where he is specializing in the career he wants to pursue and thus achieve his dreams in life. Our Great I AM, our Great God-Elohim, Jehovah-Jireh-Our Provider has provided for Moses! My work and effort in helping and guiding him in everything related to his school had been a great experience and blessing for me.

Gershom finished his career in four years, the time frame we had agreed on for him to finish. He graduated from Penn State University with a major and a minor, and he was happy that he got to attend his dream university. You may remember that when he entered this school, I was going through a divorce, in financial need, and so on. I am amazed at how hard my son worked and the many sacrifices he had to make to achieve his dream of studying for a degree at a university.

On the day of his graduation and hours before the ceremony, I visited the same place where I had dropped him off four years ago and where we had said our goodbyes. Now I was in the same place, standing with my son who had finished his degree, and we were joined by my husband and my son's father, and they were the witness to this special moment for my son and me. While standing there, I could recall that beautiful day of four years ago when we said goodbye and the difficulty we were going through as a family.

But now thanks to God, we were celebrating my son's graduation. I believe I cried for a month, the weeks before the graduation, and they were tears of joy, the joy for God's faithfulness in our lives and my son's hard work and dedication. We were celebrating that our great I Am, our great God-Elohim, Jehovah-Jireh-Our Provider had provided for Gershom's studies! My work and effort in helping and guiding him in everything related to his school had been a great experience and blessing for me.

I recognize that not every young person would trust a mother like me if they had lived and gone through what my sons have been through with me. But as you can see, thank God my sons honored me and put their trust in me, and I did not fail them because God helped me. Even though I could not avoid my failures, I am satisfied and blessed that I always fought to protect them and be with them. I thank God that my children love and value me, believe in my words, and always allow me to show them my love. I know that not every young person reacts and lives in this way, and often not even an adult can handle overcoming and live just as my children did day after day.

As you see, I love my children, and I am so proud of who they are and their accomplishments. I am excited to see all God's plans unfold in their lives. This healing and restoration in my life has given me a better relationship with my sons and has made me understand the great responsibility that they have as men in this world, and I have great respect for them. I continue to give them the best of me, which is to trust their lives in God's hands and to pray for them and help them when they need me. Now I am enjoying living as a healthy and secure mother in Christ, enjoying being a mother!

The Meaning of the Number 7

Here are the revelations of number seven for my life: This book contains seven chapters. God had instructed me to fast for seven days, and because of that, I have this book and have experienced going through the sanctification process with God. And the process of being filled with the completeness of the Holy Spirit in my life (fulfillment of God's vision) so I could write and share my life testimony. I discovered that from the first revelation I received in Germany, the one about the heart, to the last one of my seven-day fast in California the one where I fully surrender, that all this has taken seven years. All glory to God! I say glory to God that I finally surrender to him, and it is crazy to see how long it took me to be truly his. It took me seven years to know, understand, accept, and surrender my whole heart and life completely to God.

Oh, and this happened in the year 2017. This is the year I became free and complete in the Holy Spirit! I am complete by God! I am complete in Jesus Christ! For me to finally finish and write the book and submit it for publishing to the editorial company, it happened exactly on my birthday, and on that day, I turned forty-seven years of age, and my birthdate has a number seven too. At no time did I plan this but what I do know is that is not a coincidence but a divine plan. I started this book as a very broken woman, and I finished it as a complete woman who is full of the love of Christ. I had to go through this process so God could restore my life and have me experience his love and be complete by him so I could share it first at home and then with others.

I finished my first books manuscripts and managed to do it as God instructed. I wrote this book in two languages, Spanish and English, and submitted it for publication at the same time but little did I know that that would just be the beginning of my work as a writer. I thought that because God gave me this book, I would have it ready in a short time, but that was not the case. Instead, it took me a few years to finalize it because I had to learn how to become a bilingual writer. I had to learn to work on two books at the same time and to edit them, learn how to draw, how to be patience while going through many hardships and the world pandemic. The world pandemic didn't affect me but gave me the opportunity to record bible studies on youtube, facebook and minister to those that God would bring into my life while waiting on stuff for my book. The seven days of fasting and prayer were the basis for writing this book, but as you can see, that week does not encompass my whole life. In order to share my life with all its details and with a lot of transparency, it took me time to organize it and be able to narrate it in order. How much I have lived, a lifetime!

The impossible happened! I wrote this book in two languages. God saw what I could do even when I could not see it. All glory belongs to God! Drawing had never been my talent, but the Holy Spirit gave me all the visions and gifted me with drawing them for this book. This book was done just as God showed me. My dreams and visions are fulfilled, Jesus dictated, and I wrote. I have learned that because God calls, it does not mean it will be easy but hard, and the only way I could obey was to be in the completeness of the Holy Spirit, the fullness of Christ. When in need, God kept me encouraged with his Word and everything revealed during all my times with him, thank you Jehovah-Jireh, my Provider! Jesus Did

It! So, I Can Do It Too! I consider it a privilege that God has chosen me to share my life testimony to help others.

This book was supposed to be about my life, my testimony, but now I understand what this book is about. All this time I was thinking that I will have to expose my life and all the things I was ashamed of and have everyone see my life as an open book. But it was not only me whom you had to see in this book, but you had to see God the Father who became human Jesus and left us a comforter, the Holy Spirit who can fill and complete us. Through all my experiences, bad and good, God has been with me, and only by writing this book is how I discover that. Thank you, Lord! Every time God spoke to me, it was through the Holy Spirit and his Son Jesus Christ, and now I can understand how they work in our lives. I never planned or anticipated that this would be the outcome, but I can only say, "How beautiful are God's plans and how unforgettable!"

- "Pleasant words are as an honeycomb, sweet to the soul, and health to the bones" (Proverbs 16:24).
- "All scripture is given by inspiration of God, and is profitable for doctrine, for reproof, for correction, for instruction in righteousness: That the man of God may be perfect, thoroughly furnished unto all good works" (2 Timothy 3:16–17).
- "Thou hast turned for me my mourning into dancing: Thou hast put off my sackcloth and girded me with gladness; To the end that my glory may sing praise to Thee, and not be silent. O Lord my God, I will give thanks unto Thee forever" (Psalm 30:11–12).

Thank you GOD JEHOVAH-JIREH, for meeting all my needs!

Final Words

I see I was like Samson instead of Delilah. Samson is known to be a son and servant of God, his strength and life had a purpose, but his weakness was that he fell very quickly in love with women. Nothing that happened in Samson's life was wasted, even his failed love relationships had a purpose. It all worked for God's glory! So just as Samson had a purpose, I have a purpose, to share my life story and who my God is: God the Father, God the Son Jesus Christ, and God the Holy Spirit.

So now let us see what your story is. I do not know you, but I have prayed for this book and you when this book comes into your hands. It does not matter what you are doing or what you have done. God loves you and wants to bless you with his presence. My prayer is that you can use this book to help you be free from what is stopping you from living a victorious and abundant life. You can live free in Christ! Jesus Did It! And You Can Do It Too! So now I invite you to allow me to help you transform your life just as God transformed mine. And I want to do it by helping you in this process by using your Bible and this book. I hope to meet you one day and hear your testimony. God bless you!

Reader's Guide

All scripture is given by inspiration of God, and is profitable for doctrine, for reproof, for correction, for instruction in righteousness: That the man of God may be perfect, thoroughly furnished unto all good works.
—2 Timothy 3:16–17

Note: This book should not replace the Bible. So, I invite you to use your Bible as your guide first and then use this book as a tool and testimony to help you with your walk with God.

I wrote this section as a guide to help you on how to use this book. I have included my prayers. And for more help, you can visit my website at www.delilahpc.com.

How to Pray and Fast

Prayer

And the smoke of the incense, which came with the prayers of the saints, ascended up before God out of the angel's hand.
—Revelation 8:4

Prayer is talking to God. This means that is not only asking Him for help but for you to have constant communication with Him where you can listen to Him, and He can listen to you. All human beings are God's creation, but to become his child, you need to repent from your sins and accept his Son Jesus Christ as your Lord and Savior.

Our sins do have a consequence even after God has forgiven us, but we can always count on God's mercy, which stops us from getting what we really deserve. Keep communicating with the Lord even when you feel that He does not hear you. Keep praying and examining your life. If you are living according to God's will and asking according to his purpose, you can rest with the assurance that He will answer your prayer, but do not forget you just have to learn to patiently wait on his timing, not yours. More importantly is to seek his will and not yours. If God wants you to do something for Him, you will have his guidance and provision. Here are some verses that will help you with your prayers:

a. God confirms and answers prayers according to his will and purpose: 1 John 5:14, 1 Samuel 1:6–28, Acts 10:25–40

b. Meditating and praying in the Spirit: Philippians 4:6–8, Ephesians 6:18

c. Bringing your request to God: Matthew 11:28–30, Ezra 8:21–23

d. Asking according to God's will: Isaiah 58:3–14

e. Example of fasting food and how to approach God: 2 Chronicles 7:14–18; Daniel 9:3–5, 10:2–3; Matthew 6:8–18; Luke 4:2–4; Exodus 34:28; 1 Corinthians 7:3–6

f. Faith: James 1:6, Matthew 21:21

g. Help for when you do not know how to pray or cannot pray: Romans 8:26–27,34; Mark 16:19; Hebrews 7:25

h. The power of prayer and fasting: 2 Chronicles 20:1–30; James 4:7; Matthew 17:19–21

Our Father which art in heaven, Hallowed be thy name. Thy kingdom come, Thy will be done in earth, as it is in heaven. Give us this day our daily bread. And forgive us our debts, as we forgive our debtors. And lead us not into temptation, but deliver us from evil: For thine is the kingdom, and the power, and the glory, forever. Amen. Matthew 6:9b–13

Fasting

But thou, when thou fastest, anoint thine head, and wash thy face;
That thou appear not unto men to fast, but unto thy Father which is in
secret: and thy Father, which seeth in secret, shall reward thee openly.
—Matthew 6:17-18

The Bible tells us that no one should know when we are fasting because it is between God and us only. Our face must be radiant, not like we are hungry or that we have not eaten. Just as the story of Daniel and his three friends, the Bible tells us that their faces looked better than those who were eating from the King's table (Daniel 1).

In Matthew 6:17–18, these two verses show us how we should look physically. Fasting is basically offering your soul, body, and spirit to God, your whole being, and is not just about not eating or consuming small amounts of food. How you do your fast will depend on your health and desire. Seek God so you can surrender all to him and be able to give up on meals. You can even offer not to use material things such as TV, cell phones, or computers and give up being in contact with people, but to be alone with God. It is not a sacrifice to God if you offer something that you never eat or do. The fasting is not about the food; it is about having you spend time with God, dying to yourself, and being filled with his Holy Spirit.

I imagine you usually eat three meals a day and maybe between meals you eat fruit, salad, or a dessert. An example of a fast is that you can offer to not eat solid food and only drink fluids. Another example is to not eat anything and eat only at the end of your fast, but try to eat something light and do not try to make up for the meals you did not have earlier on the day. This has happened to me one time, where I ate everything I did not eat during my fast, but when I ended it, I indulged so much in food that I felt bad. If you have never fasted, I suggest you start by fasting a half-day to start with until you can do more. You may need to fast due to health issues or to lose weight, but this is not fasting for God, so remember the difference.

You may want to prepare your home before you fast. What I mean is getting your groceries done before you fast so you can avoid going to the store. This helps you avoid temptations, and it helps to have what you need at home for you and your family needs. This also helps you on staying focused on your time with God and avoid distractions. It is incredible the strength that God gives you when fasting, the power to submit your whole being to God and be satisfied with his Bread of Life. I know that not all of us have the same work schedule, so I encourage you to plan well your day of fasting and praying. Remember, your home is your first ministry. Married or single, you should have your home in order so you can spend time in your fast instead of cleaning. There are chores you cannot avoid, like the dishes, but there are some that you can, like the laundry. I suggest you fast when you are off work.

If you fast while working, it may be hard as you will not be able to focus all your attention on God. Another issue is that you may have to deal with people, and if you are feeling weak, you may get cranky and have your patience tested. So do not forget to be aware of your weakness and ask God to give you a double portion when you need it. Either way, if you are fasting from home or outside of home, I suggest you have your portions of food ready to eat and have some extras like fruits, juices, or yogurt in case you were not eating enough. Also try not to stress about eating on time as you may be hungry at a different time than the usual time. It is better to do this than finding yourself trembling with hunger or in a bad mood. A small amount of food can help you achieve your fast and thus receive the answer of God.

Focus during your fast more on praising God, and there are so many ways you can do this, like praying, meditating on who He is, worshipping through music and your voice, and reading the Bible. Let the Holy Spirit fill all your space, time, and all your being. There are so many reasons that you may need to fast. It could be that you want to spend more time with God, or you need to be delivered from strongholds or obstacles in your life. Other reasons could be you do not know what is happening in your life and need guidance or a miracle. Whatever your motive may be, it does not matter. Seek God and He will surprise you with his power and presence in your life. I made a list with suggestions of food for your fast and prayers.

Small portions: fruits, yogurt, crackers or bread, oatmeal, nuts, natural juice or shake of fruit or veggies, slices of ham, slices of cheese, vegetable salad, water as needed, hard-boiled egg, coconut juice, decaf tea/coffee to avoid having your nerves affected.

Example 1

- Breakfast: tea, four salty or sweet crackers, fruit, and water
- Lunch: one slice of bread, small veggie salad, water
- Dinner: some fruit with yogurt, water

Example 2

- Breakfast, lunch, and dinner: fruit/veggie juice or shake small cup. Drink water as needed.

Study Notes

If you have never accepted Jesus as your Savior, I invite you to accept Him by doing the prayer of salvation.

Chapter 1, Graphic 1: Carnal versus Spiritual

This chapter can help you discover what pains and sufferings you have not let go of. Also, you can use it to see in which areas of your life you are struggling with.

On a separate piece of paper, write a list of the pains and sufferings that you have not forgiven and forgotten in your life. When you are done, put this list in your open hands and give it to God by doing the following prayer, the prayer of forgiveness and healing.

Once you are done with your prayer, rip the paper into pieces and throw it in the trash. And now live believing in the healing that God has already done in your life and walk firmly in this new life.

Graphic 2: My Name, Who Am I?

On a piece of paper, write down your name and your favorite verse. Then fill it out with all your personal information. Then use it to thank God for creating you and ask him to teach you how to properly care for your whole being: spiritual, physical, and emotional.

Today You Exist!

This study can help you see God's promises for your life.

Chapter 2

This chapter can help you see how God is always present in your life.

The Door

This study can show you God's mercy and protection in your life.

Chapter 3

This chapter can help you to recognize your weaknesses and temptations and how to fix your relationship with those you have hurt. Pray this prayer, the prayer of forgiveness and healing.

Chapter 4

This chapter can help you forgive yourself and be ready for what is coming for your life.

Chapter 5

This chapter can help you not to give up on your life. Write a list of the good things you have in your life and what you have done in your life. This will help you see how God has used you to do great things in your life and can continue to use you to do so.

Chapter 6

This chapter can let you see what has happened in your life and what a powerful testimony you have!

The Shower

This study is to help you see how you should not live but remind you of how you should live in Christ.

Chapter 7

This chapter can help you go back to that first love, being Jesus's bride, how to discover your purpose in life with your talents and calling that God has given you. It should bring you awareness of God's heart for the remnant of Israel.

Graphic 3: The Groom, JESUS CHRIST

This graphic can help by exhorting you to remain committed to God and your relationship to Him as his bride.

Graphic 4: Your Position During Battle

This Bible study can help you examine who is fighting your battles in your life, you or God. This study can help see where God wants you to stand in your walk with Him, during battles or no battles.

My Song to God

This study can help you to search your heart and find the many reasons why you should praise and worship God. You may be encouraged to pray the prayer of thanksgiving.

Jesus Did It! So, I Can Do It Too!

This study can help you see that your temptations are of human nature and how to overcome them and live victoriously! So, you can live and say, "Jesus did it! So, I Can Do It Too!"

List of Prayers

1.-Prayer of Salvation

2.-Prayer of Repentance and Removal of Strongholds

3.-Prayer of Forgiveness and Healing

4.-Prayer of Surrender and Dependency on God

5.-Prayer for Obeying

6.-Prayer of Thanksgiving

7.-Prayer of Restoration

1.-Prayer of Salvation

For God so loved the world, that He gave his only begotten Son, that whosoever believeth in Him should not perish, but have everlasting life.
—John 3:16

God, I recognized that I am a sinner and that the only way to have salvation and eternal life is by repenting from all my sins and asking your Son Jesus Christ into my heart. Like your word says in John 14:6 Jesus saith unto him, I am the way, the truth, and the life: no man cometh unto the Father, but by me. Today I repent from all my sins and ask you to please forgive me for sinning against you. I accept Jesus into my heart as my Lord and Savior and accept your salvation as your word says in Romans 10:9-10 That if thou shalt confess with thy mouth the Lord Jesus, and shalt believe in thine heart that God hath raised him from the dead, thou shalt be saved. For with the heart man believeth unto righteousness; and with the mouth confession is made unto salvation. Thank you, God, that I am your child now, and in Jesus's name I pray. Amen.

2.-Prayer of Repentance and Removal of Strongholds

For the weapons of our warfare are not carnal, but mighty
through God to the pulling down of strong holds; Casting
down imaginations, and every high thing that exalteth itself
against the knowledge of God, and bringing into captivity every
thought to the obedience of Christ; And having in a readiness
to revenge all disobedience, when your obedience is fulfilled.
—2 Corinthians 10:4–6

God, your Word says in 2 Chronicles 7:14–16,

If my people, which are called by my name, shall humble themselves, and pray, and seek my face, and turn from their wicked ways; then will I hear from heaven, and will forgive their sin, and will heal their land. Now mine eyes shall be open, and mine ears attent unto the prayer that is made in this place. For now have I chosen and sanctified this house, that my name may be there forever: and mine eyes and mine heart shall be there perpetually.

I am your child, but I have disobeyed and sinned against you. My disobedience has brought much sin and strongholds into my life. I ask you to please forgive me for my disobedience and for rebelling against you. I repent for bringing idolatry and evil things into my life and for sinning against you. Please forgive me for allowing myself, others, and things to take your place in my life. Thank you, Lord, for covering all my sins with the blood of your Son Jesus Christ. With the authority I have as a child of God, I reject and cancel every stronghold, evil and filthy things that have entered my life and attacked or attached to my life, family, finances, and work. In the name of Jesus Christ, I pray. Amen.

Lord, you are my God: God the Father, God the Son Jesus Christ, and God the Holy Spirit. Your Word, the Bible, is the only authority over my life. Protect me from the enemy of my soul and from living in the flesh and help me to live in obedience to you and live filled with your Holy Spirit. Help me to memorize 2 Corinthians 10:4–6 and to be quick to apply it to my life whenever is needed. Thank you, God, for listening and your deliverance and forgiveness. In the name of Jesus, I pray. Amen.

3.-Prayer of Forgiveness and Healing

But He was wounded for our transgressions, He was
bruised for our iniquities: the chastisement of our peace
was upon Him; and with his stripes we are healed.
—Isaiah 53:5

God, today I understand that when your Son Jesus died on the cross, He took all the punishment that was due to me, and instead He offers me salvation, healing, and eternal life. I recognized that I have sinned against you by disobeying because I have not forgiven myself and those who hurt me. I have been living with unforgiveness, guilt, bitterness, anger, hurt, and much more. I had disobeyed your Word by not loving you, myself, and others. I no longer want to live with unforgiveness and lying as 1 John 4:20 says, "If a man says, I love God, and hateth his brother, he is a liar: for he that loveth not his brother whom he hath seen, how can he love God whom he hath not seen?" and Matthew 6:14–15 says, "For if ye forgive men their trespasses, your heavenly Father will also forgive you: But if ye forgive not men their trespasses, neither will your Father forgive your trespasses."

Lord, please forgive me for sinning against you. I forgive myself today and I forgive those who have offended, rejected, and hurt me. I recognized that I do not have the power to heal the brokenness that I caused to myself or someone else has caused me. I accept that those who hurt me [say the person's name aloud] cannot heal me because they are a human being just like me, but you, God, are the only one who can heal me. So, I surrender all my hurts and pains [read your list of pains and sufferings] in your hands and let it go. It is all in my past now. I accept your forgiveness, peace, and healing. Help me now to walk in obedience and humbleness so I can ask the forgiveness of those who I have hurt. Help me to not be discouraged if they do not accept my apologies and see my repented heart right away.

I recognized that only you can make them see that I am sorry for what I have done, and until they see it, I need to stay focused on following you despite them not forgiving me. I pray that the ones who have hurt me and for those who I have hurt will get to know you as Lord and Savior Jesus and experience your healing and love. Teach me how to love myself and how to protect my heart from evil. Help me to love you and to cultivate a healthy relationship with my family and others, always remembering that my heart belongs to you and only you can complete me. Fill me with your Holy Spirit and teach me how to give grace to myself and extend the same to others. Help me to enjoy this process of healing in my life, not to get impatient but to go in the process of healing that you have for me and for those I have hurt. Thank you for listening to my prayer, and I ask this in Jesus's name. Amen.

4.-Prayer of Surrender

The Lord will perfect that which concerneth me: thy mercy, O Lord, endureth forever: forsake not the works of thine own hands.
—Psalm 138:8

I Surrender My Life: God, I recognize that you created me with just one identity and needs that only you can satisfy. I pray that you give me wisdom from above so I can be guided on getting my spiritual, physical, and emotional needs met only by you. Give me discernment so I can know when Satan is tempting me by pretending to want to meet my needs. I leave my life in your hands and thank you for creating me in your image. I ask you to help me be obedient to you and live a life depending on you so you can fulfill your plans and purpose for my life. In the name of Jesus, I pray. Amen.

I Surrender My Marriage: Dear God, I believe that you created marriage and established it only between a man and a woman. The marriage is to represent Jesus Christ and the church on this earth, as your Word says in Ephesians 5:21–33. Submitting yourselves one to another in the fear of God. Wives, submit yourselves unto your own husbands, as unto the

Lord. For the husband is the head of the wife, even as Christ is the head of the church: and He is the saviour of the body. Therefore as the church is subject unto Christ, so let the wives be to their own husbands in everything. Husbands, love your wives, even as Christ also loved the church, and gave himself for it; That He might sanctify and cleanse it with the washing of water by the Word, That He might present it to himself a glorious church, not having spot, or wrinkle, or any such thing; but that it should be holy and without blemish. So ought men to love their wives as their own bodies. He that loveth his wife loveth himself. For no man ever yet hated his own flesh; but nourisheth and cherisheth it, even as the Lord the church: For we are members of his body, of his flesh, and of his bones. For this cause shall a man leave his father and mother, and shall be joined unto his wife, and they two shall be one flesh. This is a great mystery: but I speak concerning Christ and the church. Nevertheless let every one of you in particular so love his wife even as himself; and the wife see that she reverence her husband.

I surrender my marriage to you, God, so it can bring you honor and glory. I ask that you help me stay focused on my relationship with your Son Jesus despite my circumstances. Whenever I struggle with being obedient and surrendering, help me remember what you did for me at the cross so I can give that type of love to my spouse. Help me live, reminded that I am yours first before my spouse. I pray that you give us the courage to ask for help when we struggle in our marriage and guide us to know which couple is to counsel us. Protect us from evil and the enemy of our soul and from living in the flesh. Bless us and guide us with your amazing love and with the fullness of your Holy Spirit. Let your will be done in my marriage. In Jesus's name, I pray. Amen.

I Surrender My Children: God, I believe that you created us in your image and gave us the responsibility to care for the land and to procreate children. In your word in Genesis 1:28 it says: And God blessed them, and God said unto them, Be fruitful, and multiply, and replenish the earth, and subdue it: and have dominion over the fish of the sea, and over the fowl of the air, and over every living thing that moveth upon the earth. I understand that I cannot always keep my children safe from harm's way or evil things, but I know that you can protect them and keep them safe. I thank you for giving me my children, and today I surrender them to you. Help me to trust you and to remember that you love them more than I ever could. Lord, they have many needs like me too, so help me to come to you for their needs and believe that you already supplied them. Help me to work on providing the things I need as their parent and to trust you for those things I am not able to provide. Guide them in how to trust you with their whole being and protect them from evil, the enemy of their souls, and of living in the flesh. Help them to ask for prayer and help when in need and put strong believers in their life to help grow in your Word and to be encouraged. Help them to have good friends in their life, especially when in times of need. Bless and guide them with your amazing love and the fullness of your Holy Spirit. Let your will be done in their lives, and thank you for this gift of parenthood and my children. In Jesus's name, I pray. Amen.

I Surrender My Family: God, I thank you for my family and the family bonds you created. I pray that you help me love them with unconditional love and respect. I ask you to please bring healing, liberty, forgiveness, love, reconciliation, and everything needed so we can live in unity and love as a family. Help me cultivate a healthy relationship with my family whenever possible and to keep them in my prayers. Jesus, I declare you King and Savior of my family. I thank you for my extended family, and today I surrender all of them to you. Guide them on how to trust you with their whole being. Protect them from evil, the enemy of their souls, and of living in the flesh. Help them to ask for prayer and to help when in need and to put strong believers in their lives to help grow in your Word and to be encouraged. Help them to have good friends in their lives, especially in times of need. Bless them and guide them with your amazing love and with the fullness of your Holy Spirit. Let your will be done in my family. In Jesus's name, I pray. Amen.

5.-Prayer of Purpose

If ye love me, keep my commandments. And I
will pray the Father, and He shall give you another
Comforter, that He may abide with you forever.
—John 14:15-16

Dear Lord, I pray that you show me the Christian church where I can attend and be part of it. Help me obey your commandments and organize my daily life so I can spend time with you through the reading of your Word, the Bible, in prayer and the other ways I need to. I recognize that you made me a human being with one identity and three urgent needs—physical, emotional, and spiritual. Please give me the wisdom from above so I know how to go about having you meet my needs so I can know where to look, ask, and seek in times of need. Show me the people that you have placed in my life to help me with my spiritual growth and other aspects of my life. Reveal my talents and calling so I can serve you and bring you glory. When I need direction, clarity, or the ability to overcome trials, help me to pray and fast so I can hear your voice and have faith in you and your plans, for your Word says in Jeremiah 29:11-12, "For I know the thoughts that I think toward you, saith the LORD, thoughts of peace, and not of evil, to give you an expected end. Then shall ye call upon me, and ye shall go and pray unto me, and I will hearken unto you."

Thank you, Lord, for allowing me to be in your presence and for the freedom I have in you. Thank you for letting me know that there is only purpose in obedience. I desire to fulfill my purpose, just like your son Jesus did. Let your will be done in my life. In Jesus's name, I pray this. Amen.

6.-Prayer of Gratitude

I will praise thee; for I am fearfully and wonderfully made:
marvellous are thy works; and that my soul knoweth right well.
—Psalm 139:14

Dear God, I thank you for my life and for creating me in your image. Thank you for all the blessings that I have in my life:

_____

_____

_____

_____

7.-Prayer of Restoration: Declaring God's Blessings Over My Life

Dear God, I thank you for your faithfulness and for always loving me. I do not deserve any of your blessings, but because you are merciful, God, you choose to bless me. Thank you for this abundant life and for giving me blessings for obeying you. I declare them over my life. In Jesus's name, I pray. Amen.

And it shall come to pass, if thou shalt hearken diligently unto the voice of the Lord thy God, to observe and to do all his commandments which I command thee this day, that the Lord thy God will set thee on high above all nations of the earth: And all these blessings shall come on thee, and overtake thee, if thou shalt hearken unto the voice of the Lord thy God. Blessed shalt thou be in the city, and blessed shalt thou be in the field. Blessed shall be the fruit of thy body, and the fruit of thy ground, and the fruit of thy cattle, the increase of thy kine, and the flocks of thy sheep. Blessed shall be thy basket and thy store. Blessed shalt thou be when thou comest in, and blessed shalt thou be when thou goest out. The Lord shall cause thine enemies that rise up against thee to be smitten before thy face: they shall come out against thee one way, and flee before thee seven ways. The Lord shall command the blessing upon thee in thy storehouses, and in all that thou settest thine hand unto; and he shall bless thee in the land which the Lord thy God giveth thee. The Lord shall establish thee an holy people unto himself, as he hath sworn unto thee, if thou shalt keep the commandments of the Lord thy God, and walk in his ways. And all people of the earth shall see that thou art called by the name of the Lord; and they shall be afraid of thee. And the Lord shall make thee plenteous in goods, in the fruit of thy body, and in the fruit of thy cattle, and in the fruit of thy ground, in the land which the Lord sware unto thy fathers to give thee. The Lord shall open unto thee his good treasure, the heaven to give the rain unto thy land in his season, and to bless all the work of thine hand: and thou shalt lend unto many nations, and thou shalt not borrow. And the Lord shall make thee the head, and not the tail; and thou shalt be above only, and thou shalt not be beneath; if that thou hearken unto the commandments of the Lord thy God, which I command thee this day, to observe and to do them: And thou shalt not go aside from any of the words which I command thee this day, to the right hand, or to the left, to go after other gods to serve them. (Deuteronomy 28:1–14)

Blessed is the man that walketh not in the counsel of the ungodly, nor standeth in the way of sinners, nor sitteth in the seat of the scornful. But his delight is in the law of the LORD; and in his law doth he meditate day and night. And he shall be like a tree planted by the rivers of water, that bringeth forth his fruit in his season; his leaf also shall not wither; and whatsoever he doeth shall prosper. (Psalm 1:1–3)

The LORD bless thee and keep thee: The LORD make his face shine upon thee and be gracious unto thee: The LORD lift up his countenance upon thee and give thee peace. And they shall put my name upon the children of Israel, and I will bless them. (Numbers 6:24–27)

Printed in the United States
by Baker & Taylor Publisher Services